CW0054429G

CONNECTING HISTORY

National 4 & 5

The Atlantic Slave Trade,

1770–1807

Eleanor Trevena

Boost

HODDER
GIBSON
AN HACHETTE UK COMPANY

The Publishers would like to thank the following for permission to reproduce copyright material.

Picture credits – please see page viii.

Acknowledgements

pp.13 & 60 two extracts from *Black Ivory: Slavery in the British Empire* by James Walvin, published by Blackwell Publishers Ltd. Copyright © James Walvin 1992, 2001. Reproduced with permission of the Licensor through PLSclear; **p.14** extract from p.96 of *Fighting the Slave Trade: West African Strategies* by Sylviane A. Diouf, published by Boydell and Brewer Limited, 2004. Copyright © 2003 Sylviane A. Diouf; **pp.20 & 105** two extracts from *The Slave Trade: The History of the Atlantic Slave Trade 1440–1870*, by Hugh Thomas. Copyright © Hugh Thomas, 1997, used by permission of The Wylie Agency (UK) Limited; **pp.36, 72 & 91** three extracts from *Bury the Chains: The British Struggle to Abolish Slavery* by Adam Hochschild, published by Macmillan. Copyright © Adam Hochschild 2005. Reproduced with permission of the Licensor through PLSclear; **pp.47 & 66** two extracts from *White Fury: A Jamaican Slaveholder and the Age of Revolution* by Christer Petley, published by Oxford University Press, 2018. Copyright © Christer Petley 2018. Reproduced with permission of the Licensor through PLSclear; **p.58** extract from *Surviving Slavery in the British Caribbean* by Randy M. Browne, published by University of Pennsylvania Press, Inc. 2017; **p.90** extract from *A Short History of Slavery* by James Walvin, published by Penguin. Copyright © James Walvin, 2007. Reprinted by permission of Penguin Books Limited; **p.100** extract from *Revolutionary Emancipation: Slavery and Abolitionism in the British West Indies* by Claudius K. Fergus. Published by Louisiana State University Press, 2013; **p.105** extract from *Empire: How Britain Made the Modern World* by Niall Ferguson, published by Allen Lane. Copyright © Niall Ferguson, 2003. Reprinted by permission of Penguin Books Limited; **p.105** extract from *The Trader, The Owner, The Slave: Parallel Lives in the Age of Slavery* by James Walvin, published by Jonathan Cape. Copyright © James Walvin, 2007. Reprinted by permission of The Random House Group Limited; **p.107** extract from *Black and British: A Forgotten History* by David Olusoga. Published by Pan Macmillan, 2016. Reproduced with permission of the Licensor through PLSclear.

Every effort has been made to trace all copyright holders, but if any have been inadvertently overlooked, the Publishers will be pleased to make the necessary arrangements at the first opportunity.

Although every effort has been made to ensure that website addresses are correct at time of going to press, Hodder Gibson cannot be held responsible for the content of any website mentioned in this book. It is sometimes possible to find a relocated web page by typing in the address of the home page for a website in the URL window of your browser.

Hachette UK's policy is to use papers that are natural, renewable and recyclable products and made from wood grown in well-managed forests and other controlled sources. The logging and manufacturing processes are expected to conform to the environmental regulations of the country of origin.

Orders: please contact Hachette UK Distribution, Hely Hutchinson Centre, Milton Road, Didcot, Oxfordshire, OX11 7HH. Telephone: +44 (0)1235 827827. Email education@hachette.co.uk Lines are open from 9 a.m. to 5 p.m., Monday to Friday. You can also order through our website: www.hoddereducation.co.uk. If you have queries or questions that aren't about an order, you can contact us at hoddergibson@hodder.co.uk

© Eleanor Trevena 2023
First published in 2023 by
Hodder Gibson, an imprint of Hodder Education
An Hachette UK Company
50 Frederick Street
Edinburgh, EH2 1EX

Impression number	5	4	3	2	1
Year	2027	2026	2025	2024	2023

All rights reserved. Apart from any use permitted under UK copyright law, no part of this publication may be reproduced or transmitted in any form or by any means, electronic or mechanical, including photocopying and recording, or held within any information storage and retrieval system, without permission in writing from the publisher or under licence from the Copyright Licensing Agency Limited. Further details of such licences (for reprographic reproduction) may be obtained from the Copyright Licensing Agency Limited, www.cla.co.uk

Cover photo © National Museums Liverpool/Bridgeman Images
Illustrations by Integra Software Services Pvt. Ltd., Pondicherry, India and Aptara, Inc. (pages 2-3)
Typeset by Integra Software Services Pvt. Ltd., Pondicherry, India
Produced by DZS Grafik, Printed in Slovenia

A catalogue record for this title is available from the British Library.

ISBN: 978 1 3983 4539 3

MIX
Paper | Supporting responsible forestry
FSC™ C104740
www.fsc.org

SCOTLAND EXCEL

We are an approved supplier on the Scotland Excel framework.

Find us on your school's procurement system as **Hachette UK Distribution Ltd** or **Hodder & Stoughton Limited t/a Hodder Education.**

Contents

Welcome to Connecting History!

The aim of this series is to provide rich and accessible information that will help learners, teachers and lecturers to get the most out of History. The series has dedicated resources for National 4/ National 5 and Higher History. It sparks interest, provides the right level of detailed information and is straightforward to access through its consistent and clear structure.

Overall, Connecting History is designed to provide a fresh approach to the study of History. The series is:

- **Consistent.** The content of each book is structured in a similar way around the key themes of the course. This clear structure will make it easy to find what you need when studying History. Indeed, all books in the series are designed this way, so that every book, for every unit, is equally accessible. This will make it quick and easy to find the information that learners and teachers need, whether revising, extending study or planning a lesson.
- **Focused.** Up-to-date course specifications have been used to create these books. This means that it is easy for learners and teachers to find information and provides assurance that the books offer complete coverage of the examinations, as well as general study. This means that you will not have to read through multiple long texts to collate information for one content area – our authors have done this already.
- **Relevant.** The importance and significance of each area to your understanding of our world and history has been clearly set out. Background sections in each chapter capture issues in their entirety, and sub-sections go into detail on key issues, with a number of sources and interpretations included. These texts go beyond the standard material that has been in circulation for a while and bring in new opinions, evidence and historical scholarship to enrich the study of History. We hope that this will continue to foster not only an ability to be highly successful in History, but also to inspire a love of the subject.
- **For today.** These units are not just about the past, they are about today. Themes of social justice, equality, change and power are all discussed. The most up-to-date research has been reflected by our authors, old interpretations have been challenged and we have taken a fresh look at the importance of each unit. We firmly believe that it is impossible to understand the present without a firm understanding of the past.
- **For tomorrow.** This series prepares learners for the future. It provides the knowledge, understanding and skills needed to be highly successful in History exams. Perhaps just as importantly, these books help learners to be critical and curious in their engagement with History. They challenge readers to go beyond the most obvious or traditional narratives and get to the bottom of the meaning and importance of the past. These skills will make readers not only successful learners, but also effective and responsible citizens going forward.

We hope that you enjoy using the Connecting History series and that it fosters a love of History, as well as exam success.

Several units in this series are supported by digital resources for planning, revision, extension and assessment in Boost, our online learning platform. These will be updated annually to reflect recent course and assessment updates. If the nature of the assessment changes, or the skills are tweaked, fear not, our digital resources will be updated to reflect this. To find out more about this series – including the Boost resources and eBooks – visit **www.hoddergibson.co.uk/connecting-history**

Our academic reviewers

Every Connecting History textbook has been reviewed by a member of our Academic Review Panel. This panel, co-ordinated by our Academic Advisory Board, consists of nine Academic Editors with links to the University of Glasgow across a range of historical specialisms.

Each Academic Editor reviewed our texts to ensure that the:

o historiography is in line with the latest research and scholarship
o content is culturally appropriate, up to date and inclusive
o material is accurate and states facts clearly.

Dr Shantel George is a lecturer in History, researching the transatlantic slave trade, slavery and emancipation, with a particular focus on the British Caribbean. She received her PhD from SOAS, University of London, and is currently finishing a book manuscript, *"Yoruba are on a Rock": Liberated Africans and African Work in Grenada* (under contract with Cambridge University Press).

Academic Review Panel	Units reviewed
Professor Dauvit Broun, Professor of Scottish History	Higher: The Wars of Independence, 1249–1328 National 4 & 5: The Wars of Independence, 1286–1328
Dr Rosemary Elliot, Senior Lecturer (Economic & Social History)	Higher: The Impact of the Great War, 1914–1928 National 4 & 5: The Era of the Great War, 1900–1928
Dr Shantel George, Lecturer in Transatlantic Slavery (History)	National 4 & 5: The Atlantic Slave Trade, 1770–1807
Dr Ewan Gibbs, Lecturer in Global Inequalities (Economic & Social History)	Higher: Britain, 1851–1951
Dr Lizanne Henderson, Senior Lecturer in History (Interdisciplinary Studies)	Higher: Migration and Empire, 1830–1939 National 4 & 5: Migration and Empire, 1830–1939
Dr Mark McLay, Lecturer in American History	Higher: USA, 1918–1968 National 4 & 5: Free at Last? Civil Rights in the USA, 1918–1968
Dr Alexander Marshall, Senior Lecturer (History)	Higher: Russia, 1881–1921 National 4 & 5: Red Flag: Lenin and the Russian Revolution, 1894–1921
Professor Ray Stokes, Chair of Business History (Economic & Social History)	Higher: Germany, 1815–1939
Dr Danielle Willard-Kyle, Research Associate	National 4 & 5: Hitler and Nazi Germany, 1919–1939

Academic Advisory Board	Professor Karin Bowie, Professor of Early Modern Scottish History, University of Glasgow
	Dr Philip Tonner, Lecturer in Education (History), University of Glasgow

Introduction

The transatlantic slave trade was the largest forced migration in human history. Historians have calculated that, between 1514 and 1866, there were more than 36,000 slave voyages across the Atlantic Ocean. These voyages transported over 12 million captive people from Africa to the colonies of the Caribbean and the wider Americas. As many as 2 million Africans died during the journey. For those who landed in the 'New World', slavery meant a life of unimaginable suffering.

Britain played a leading role in the slave trade. Between the middle of the seventeenth century and the abolition of the British slave trade in 1807, British ships carried over 3.4 million Africans into enslavement. This topic focuses on the period between 1770 and 1807. During these years, individuals and organisations in Britain and its colonies made huge profits from the forced labour of enslaved Africans.

What is enslavement?

Forms of enslavement have existed since ancient times. Slavery is people exploiting people by entrapping them and depriving them of their freedom. It has taken different forms, but typically involves forcing people to work without pay and in harsh conditions. Slavery has always existed and still does.

The particular type of slavery that you will learn about in this topic was a global institution that involved Europeans exploiting the forced labour of Africans to make huge profits. Slavery, as operated by the European powers, was a form of **chattel enslavement**. This means that the people who were enslaved were treated as property and could be bought and sold at the whim of their enslavers. It was also race-based and hereditary, meaning that the children of enslaved people were born with enslaved status.

Enslaved people were the first to fight against the slave trade, through acts of resistance. At the start of the period we are studying, few people in Britain questioned the morality of the slave trade. Yet by the end of the eighteenth century, a movement emerged in Britain that aimed to put an end to it completely. The campaign achieved success in 1807 with the Act for the Abolition of the Slave Trade. It is important to note that illegal slave trading continued for decades after this and slavery itself was not abolished in the British Empire until 1833.

In June 2020, Members of the European Parliament backed a resolution calling on the European Union to recognise the slave trade as a 'crime against humanity' and to make 2 December the European Day commemorating the abolition of the slave trade.

In this book you will learn about the organisation and nature of the slave trade, and its impact on Britain, the Caribbean and Africa. You will learn about the experience of captives in the 'slave factories' on the African coast and the horrific conditions they experienced on board the ships that carried them across the Atlantic Ocean. You will discover the traumatic nature of daily life for enslaved people on the plantations of the Caribbean. You will examine the ways in which enslaved people resisted and how their enslavers responded to these acts of resistance. Lastly, you will learn about the reasons why the slave trade was ended in 1807.

Note

Language

When studying this topic, it is **vital** to pay attention to language and how it is used.

Primary sources often describe enslaved people using words and terms that we now know to be offensive. These terms have been avoided where possible or, if used, they are explained in the Glossary section.

We have, for the most part, used 'enslaved person/people' over 'slave/s', where possible, except when used in primary sources and by historians, or when it would make the text too repetitive and difficult to understand. We have also retained instances that specifically link to the SQA's key issues, so the assessment connection is clear to students.

The word 'enslaved' highlights the fact that African people were **forcibly** placed and held in the condition of slavery, whereas the term 'slave' suggests that slavery was their natural condition. Similarly, participants in acts of resistance against the slave system are referred to as 'freedom fighters', 'anti-slavery activists' or 'abolitionists'.

We use the word 'captive' as this is defined as a 'person who is enslaved, dominated or imprisoned'. This appropriately conveys that captives were indeed prisoners, captured and held against their will.

One final point of note: The slave trade is a very broad topic, and it would be impossible to cover everything in one course. This book specifically examines the period between 1770 and 1807. It focuses on the British slave trade and its impact on Britain, west and west-central Africa, and the Caribbean.

Whether revising for an N4 or N5 assessment, or deepening your understanding of a particular area, this book will help you.

Each chapter covers a specific issue that might appear as an N4/5 assessment item, and the information contained in the following pages will support you in writing a powerful response.

Good luck!

 Note

Sensitive content

Readers should be aware that a few sections of this textbook include content which may prompt distress in some people. Any sections containing such content will show a sensitive content box on the page, like the one shown here on the right.

CAUTION: SENSITIVE CONTENT

However, readers should bear in mind that the subject matter as a whole covers themes such as racism, torture and abuse, and so there will be sections throughout containing challenging material. These sections may be equally upsetting and affect people differently, depending on their individual lived experiences.

The Publishers would like to thank the following for permission to reproduce copyright material.

Photo credits

p.v reviewer's own; **p.1 (detail)** © Heritage-Images/TopFoto; **p.3 (left)** © Sabena Jane Blackbird/Alamy Stock Photo, **(right)** © milicenta/stock.adobe.com; **p.4** © National Museums Liverpool/Bridgeman Images; **p.7** © Chronicle/Alamy Stock Photo; **p.8** © Martin Fowler/Shutterstock.com; **p.9** © marc zakian 2/Alamy Stock Photo; **p.11** © anphotos99/stock.adobe.com; **p.12** © jbdodane/Alamy Stock Photo; **p.13** © Granger/Bridgeman Images; **p.19 (top)** © atosan/stock.adobe.com, **(bottom)** © Sura Nualpradid/stock.adobe.com; **p.23** © Heritage-Images/TopFoto; **p.25** © CORBIS/Corbis via Getty Images; **p.32 (detail)** © Chronicle of World History/Alamy Stock Photo; **p.33** © PA Images/Alamy Stock Photo; **p.35** © MrPreecha/stock.adobe.com; **p.36** © Chronicle of World History/Alamy Stock Photo; **p.37** © James/stock.adobe.com; **p.39** © Debbie Ann Powell/stock.adobe.com; **p.40 (top)** © Ian Dagnall/Alamy Stock Photo, **(bottom)** © Debbie Ann Powell/stock.adobe.com; **p.41** © Debbie Ann Powell/stock.adobe.com; **p.43 (top)** © Juulijs/stock.adobe.com, **(bottom)** © Izzy/stock.adobe.com; **p.45** © Oswald Hall, Auchincruive via Wikimedia Commons © Creative Commons Attribution Share-alike license 2.0; **p.46** © Eric Begbie/Alamy Stock Photo; **p.54 (detail)** © johan10/stock.adobe.com; **p.56** © nyiragongo/stock.adobe.com; **p.57** © Sergey Kohl/stock.adobe.com; **p.61** © Chronicle/Alamy Stock Photo; **p.62** © Wollwerth Imagery/stock.adobe.com; **p.64** © Wilberforce House Museum/Bridgeman Images; **p.65** © Richard Cummins/Alamy Stock Photo; **p.70** © johan10/stock.adobe.com; **p.71 (top)** © Prachaya Roekdeethaweesab/Shutterstock.com, **(bottom)** © The Granger Collection/Alamy Stock Photo; **p.77 (detail)** © AF Fotografie/Alamy Stock Photo; **p.79** © Artefact/Alamy Stock Photo; **p.80** © Pictorial Press Ltd/Alamy Stock Photo; **p.81** © Granger Historical Picture Archive/Alamy Stock Photo; **p.85** © Pictorial Press Ltd/Alamy Stock Photo; **p.91** © AF Fotografie/Alamy Stock Photo; **p.92** © Granger, NYC/TopFoto; **p.93** © simon leigh/Alamy Stock Photo; **p.95** © IanDagnall Computing/Alamy Stock Photo; **p.96** © The Picture Art Collection/Alamy Stock Photo; **p.97** © Whitworth Art Gallery/Bridgeman Images; **p.106** © Pictorial Press Ltd/Alamy Stock Photo

Chapter 1

The Triangular Trade

The aim of this chapter is to establish how the slave trade operated. It will explain the 'triangular' nature of the slave trade and highlight what happened at each stage of the triangle.

It will examine the impact of the slave trade on British ports, African societies and Caribbean plantations. It will explore the conditions experienced by captives in the 'slave factories' on the African coast. Finally, it will discuss the conditions experienced by captives on board the ships that transported them across the Atlantic Ocean.

Together, this will allow you to respond to questions from Key issue 1: The Triangular Trade.

Link to the assessment

National 4 and 5

Key issue 1: The Triangular Trade

- The organisation and nature of the slave trade
- The effects of the slave trade on British ports
- The effects of the slave trade on African societies
- The effects of the slave trade on Caribbean plantations
- 'Slave factories' on the African coast
- The economics and conditions of the 'Middle Passage'

 **Note**

The SQA course specification refers to 'The effects of the slave trade on West Indian plantations.' The term 'West Indies' is outdated. Instead, 'Caribbean' is used throughout this book.

Background

During the 400 years in which the Atlantic slave trade operated, more than 12 million people were taken from their homes in Africa and sold to European traders. They were transported across the Atlantic Ocean to **colonies** in the Caribbean and the wider Americas. Here, their forced labour was used to produce goods that were sold in Europe for huge profits.

How did the slave trade begin?

Europeans first came to west Africa in the early fifteenth century, searching for new trade routes to the East. They discovered the wealth of the continent and began trading in products such as gold, ivory and spices. They also began trading in people.

The Portuguese were the first Europeans to trade in enslaved Africans. They were quickly followed by other European countries, including Britain.

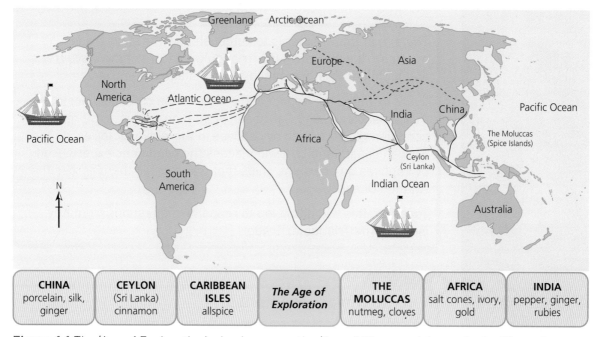

| CHINA porcelain, silk, ginger | CEYLON (Sri Lanka) cinnamon | CARIBBEAN ISLES allspice | *The Age of Exploration* | THE MOLUCCAS nutmeg, cloves | AFRICA salt cones, ivory, gold | INDIA pepper, ginger, rubies |

Figure 1.1 The 'Age of Exploration', also known as the 'Age of Discovery', began in the fifteenth century and continued into the seventeenth century. During this period Europeans began exploring the world in search of new trade routes. This was the period in which the Atlantic slave trade began.

How did Britain become involved in the slave trade?

In 1562, an English adventurer called John Hawkins set sail from England to Sierra Leone with three ships. Off the coast of Sierra Leone, he captured 300 Africans and took them to the Spanish colony of Hispaniola, in modern-day Haiti and the Dominican Republic. Upon arrival, he sold the captives to the Spanish settlers. Hawkins made so much money from his voyages that he was subsequently sponsored by Queen Elizabeth I of England, who provided him with ships, supplies and guns.

In 1663, a **Royal Charter** established the Company of Royal Adventurers of England trading with Africa. Shareholders included King Charles II and his brother, the Duke of York, who later became King James II. The company was renamed the Royal African Company in 1672. Between the 1670s and the 1730s, the Royal African Company transported around 150,000 African men, women and children into slavery. This was more than any other British company in the whole history of the Atlantic slave trade.

By the period 1770–1807, Britain had become the dominant slave-trading power. Other European powers who were involved in the slave trade were Portugal, Spain, France, the Netherlands, Denmark and Sweden. In this topic we will focus on the role of Britain.

1.1 The organisation and nature of the slave trade

The Atlantic slave trade is also sometimes referred to as the 'Triangular Trade'. Broadly speaking, the trade followed a triangular pattern, as shown in Figure 1.2. There were three main stages: the journey from Britain to Africa, the voyage from Africa to the Caribbean and the return journey from the Caribbean back to Britain.

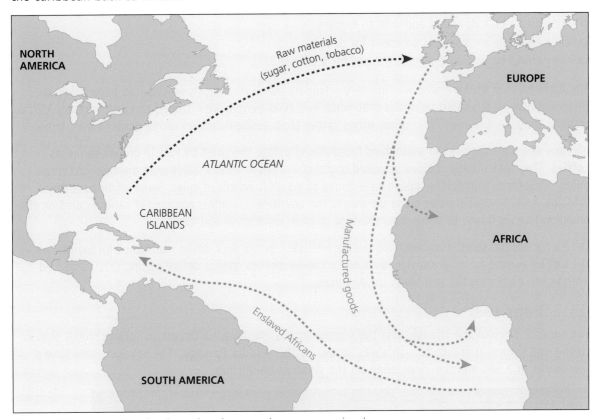

Figure 1.2 A map showing how the slave trade was organised

1.1.1 Stage one

The first stage of the triangle involved ships sailing from ports such as Liverpool to the west coast of Africa. These ships were loaded with trade goods that would be exchanged for captive Africans once the ships arrived on the African coast. Typical trade goods included glass beads, cloth, metals, alcohol and weapons (Figure 1.3). Traders would also import large quantities of shells, typically cowrie shells, to use as a means of payment for enslaved people (Figure 1.4).

Figure 1.3 Glass beads used in slave trading. In west and west-central Africa, millions of these beads were traded for people.

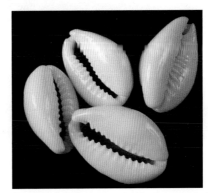

Figure 1.4 Cowrie shells from the Maldives in the Indian Ocean were one of the major forms of currency across west Africa from the thirteenth to the nineteenth centuries

On the coast, British traders paid taxes and offered gifts to local African traders who controlled the supply of captives. They also established trading posts, known as 'slave factories' or 'slave castles'. You will learn more about the slave factories later in this chapter.

Forms of enslavement

People could become enslaved in Africa in a number of ways:

- they could be kidnapped and sold to traders
- they could be enslaved as payment for debts
- they could be enslaved as punishment for a crime.

The main form of enslavement was military – traders purchased captives who had been taken as prisoners of war. It should be noted that when enslaved people were traded to Europeans by African traders, they were usually from other tribes rather than being members of the trader's own tribe.

Africans who were captured or sold inland faced a long trek to the coast on foot in groups known as **coffles.** They were usually chained or **yoked** together in twos or threes. Some were marched just a few miles, while those from further inland were forced to march hundreds of miles. Some might have been sold and re-sold multiple times along the way to the coastline. Countless numbers of captives died on the gruelling journey inland to shore, from shortage of food, exhaustion and illness.

Once on board the ships, many enslaved people were kept below deck, often imprisoned for months while the captain waited for other consignments or for the weather to change before setting sail. Some died even before beginning the journey to the Americas.

1.1.2 Stage two

The second stage of the triangle was the voyage across the Atlantic Ocean on sailing ships, similar to the one shown in Figure 1.5. This was known as the **'Middle Passage'**. The voyage could take a few weeks or a few months, depending on the weather conditions.

Figure 1.5 This painting of a Liverpool slave ship by the artist William Jackson dates from around 1780. Note the four ventilation ports in the lower hull of the ship. This was the part of the ship in which captives were held during the voyage across the Atlantic Ocean.

Preparing the captives for sale

On reaching the Caribbean territories the captives were 'prepared' so that they could be sold. They were washed and their sores and wounds were covered up to make them look healthier, so that they would fetch a higher price. They were sold, either at **auction** to the highest bidder or in a **scramble**. A scramble was a type of sale in which the captives were kept together in an enclosure. Buyers paid a fixed sum in advance and, on a signal, rushed in and grabbed the captives they wanted.

Olaudah Equiano, a former enslaved person who later became an anti-slavery activist, described how he was sold in a scramble when he first arrived in the Caribbean:

Source 1.1

On a signal given, such as the beat of a drum, the buyers rush at once into the yard where the slaves are confined, and make choice of that parcel they like best. The noise and clamour with which this is attended, and the eagerness visible on the countenances of the buyers, serve not a little to increase the apprehensions of the terrified Africans.

Olaudah Equiano (1789) *The Interesting Narrative of the Life of Olaudah Equiano, or Gustavus Vassa, The African*

Selling the captives

The healthiest captives were sold quickly, but it could be days or even weeks before those who were weaker were sold. Captives who were not sold or who were too ill upon arrival, the so-called 'refuse slaves', were often left to die unattended on the quayside of the port. They could also be sold at auction or transported on to other territories.

The enslaved Africans who had been sold were taken to **plantations**. Here they were forced to harvest the crops and produce the consumer goods that were in demand in Britain, such as sugar, cotton and rum. They might also be forced to work as domestic servants for their enslavers.

 Note

The most important of all the consumer goods produced on the plantations of the Caribbean was sugar. You will learn more about the importance of sugar in the next chapter.

1.1.3 Stage three

The third stage of the triangle involved ships sailing back to Britain loaded with the consumer goods produced by enslaved Africans.

The full cycle of an Atlantic slave-trade voyage could last up to eighteen months. Other journeys directly across the Atlantic were made to supply the Caribbean with goods produced in Britain, such as beef, salted fish, clothing and copper stills for distilling sugar. Ships also transported goods to supply the homes of enslavers, such as furniture, books and wine.

Key fact summary

The organisation and nature of the slave trade
The Atlantic slave trade followed a triangular route, from Britain to Africa, then from Africa to the Caribbean, and from the Caribbean back to Britain.
The first stage of the triangle was the journey from Britain to Africa, in ships loaded with trade goods such as cloth, metals and alcohol.
In Africa, trade goods were exchanged for captive Africans.
Captive Africans were transported across the Atlantic Ocean in ships – this part of the triangle was known as the 'Middle Passage'.

In the Caribbean, captive Africans were sold, either at auction or in a scramble.

Enslaved people were forced to work on plantations to produce the consumer goods that were in demand in Britain, such as sugar, cotton and rum. The most important of these was sugar.

The final stage of the triangle involved ships sailing back to Britain loaded with the consumer goods that were produced on plantations.

Activities

1 a) Sketch or print a map of the Triangular Trade, similar to that shown in Figure 1.2. Place the map on a larger sheet of paper so that you have a large area of space around the edges of your map.

 b) Using the information about how the slave trade was organised, annotate your map, labelling it to show what happened at each stage of the 'triangle'.

2 Use the information from your map to write a detailed paragraph about how the trade in enslaved people operated. You should aim to write an answer which includes several points. Write each point in a separate sentence.
(Hint: you might choose to describe what happened at each stage of the 'triangle'.)

3 a) Read Source 1.1 again. In this source, Olaudah Equiano describes how he was sold in a 'scramble' upon arrival in the Caribbean.

 b) Give at least two points of information from the source to explain what happened during a scramble.

1.2 The effects of the slave trade on British ports

The three main British slave-trading ports were:

- London until the 1730s
- Bristol from the 1730s until the 1740s
- Liverpool from the 1740s until the end of the slave trade in 1807.

Other British ports were also involved in the slave trade, albeit on a smaller scale. These included Devon ports such as Barnstaple and Plymouth, coastal towns such as Whitehaven in Cumbria and Scottish ports such as Greenock and Port Glasgow. Lancaster was Britain's fourth largest slave-trading port. In 1771, ships from Lancaster carried 950 African captives into slavery.

Investment and employment in the ports

In the ports there was huge investment in quaysides, warehouses and factories, in addition to employment for carpenters, rope makers, dock workers and sailors. Jobs could also be found in inns and taverns that were built near the docks.

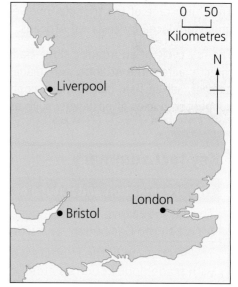

Figure 1.6 The three main British slave-trading ports

This section will explore the impact of the slave trade on London, Bristol and Liverpool.

1.2.1 The impact of the slave trade on London

In total, London-based vessels carried more than 800,000 Africans into a life of slavery. Despite being overtaken in importance first by Bristol and then by Liverpool, the city of London continued to send ships to west Africa until the end of the British slave trade in 1807. In 1771 alone, 58 London-based ships transported 8000 captives from Africa to the Americas.

One influential London-based merchant at the end of the eighteenth century was Richard Miles. Between 1772 and 1780, Miles kept detailed records of 1308 exchanges that he made for captives on the Gold Coast of Africa.

London itself grew as a result of its involvement in the trade in enslaved people. For example, the West India Docks (Figure 1.7), which opened in 1802, were built partly to provide warehouses for the storage of goods from the trade with the Caribbean.

London also became the headquarters of the banks and insurance companies that financed the slave trade voyages. You will learn more about these in the next chapter.

Figure 1.7 The West India Docks, London. The import and export docks together enclosed 54 acres of water and had a 21-year monopoly on trade with the Caribbean.

1.2.2 The impact of the slave trade on Bristol

Up to 1807, there were over 2000 separate slave-trading voyages to Africa from Bristol. This was about 19 per cent of the total from British ports. In 1771, 23 Bristol ships transported nearly 9000 Africans into slavery.

The slave trade was important to Bristol's economy. In 1789, it is estimated that the trade to Africa and the Caribbean made up over 80 per cent of the total value of Bristol's trade abroad.

Many residents and businesses of Bristol made money from the trade in enslaved people. Local factories produced **copper sheathing** for slave ships and made goods to trade in Africa, such as bottles, pots and pans, glass ornaments and gunpowder.

Figure 1.8 The historic Queen Square, Bristol, was built between 1619 and 1727. It was home to wealthy merchants and enslavers who made money from the forced labour of Africans in the Caribbean.

1.2.3 The impact of the slave trade on Liverpool

The first recorded slave ship to set sail from Liverpool was the *Liverpool Merchant*. In 1700 the *Liverpool Merchant* carried more than 200 captives from Africa to Barbados. By 1740, there were 33 ships a year leaving Liverpool.

From the 1740s until the end of the British slave trade in 1807, Liverpool was the most important slave-trading port (Figure 1.9). In the two decades before the abolition of the slave trade, Liverpool was responsible for 75 per cent of all slave-trading voyages across Europe. Liverpool dominated the trade to such an extent that one in five African captives crossing the Atlantic Ocean was carried in a Liverpool slave ship. Some key points about Liverpool's involvement in the trade in enslaved people are explained below.

○ As a result of the slave trade, Liverpool became a world leader in shipbuilding and rapidly transformed from a small town into a major port. In 1700, Liverpool had a population of 5000. By 1800, its population had increased to 78,000.

○ Liverpool benefited financially from its involvement in the trade in enslaved people. Local craftspeople and industries supplied the slave ships. These industries included linen, glass, leather and metal goods.

○ Estimates suggest that one in eight of Liverpool's population depended on trade with Africa and 40 per cent of the port's income came from the slave trade.

○ Many prominent individuals in Liverpool made their fortunes from the slave trade. In the years between 1787 and 1807, all of Liverpool's mayors were involved in the trading of enslaved people. In 1807, Thomas Leyland, a Liverpool slave merchant, founded Leyland and Bullins bank. Through various amalgamations, this bank eventually became part of HSBC.

Expansion of trade

The growth in importance of Liverpool as a slave-trading port had a knock-on effect on towns in the surrounding area. Liverpool provided an outlet for Manchester's cotton goods. In 1739, Manchester's export trade was £14,000 a year. By 1779 it was over £300,000. A third of this business went to Africa, while half went to either the Caribbean or the North American colonies.

Figure 1.9 The legacy of Liverpool's involvement in the trade in enslaved people is visible today throughout the city. Liverpool's Town Hall, dating from 1749, has a decorative frieze on the exterior showing African elephants, crocodiles and lions.

Using this information in your assessment

This section gives some background information to provide context for your study of the impact of the slave trade on British ports. When answering questions on this topic, you should ensure that the examples you use are from the years 1770 to 1807.

Key fact summary

The effects of the slave trade on British ports
London was the home of the banks and insurance companies that financed the slave trade.
Factories in Bristol benefited financially from production of goods to trade in Africa.
In the period 1770–1807, Liverpool was the main British slave-trading port.

Liverpool became a world leader in shipbuilding.
Manchester benefited financially from the ability to sell its cotton goods via the nearby port of Liverpool.
Other British ports that were involved in the trade in enslaved people included Lancaster, Plymouth and Port Glasgow.
Many jobs were created in the ports as a result of the slave trade, including dock workers, sailors, carpenters and rope makers.

Activities

4 Research the role of either London, Bristol or Liverpool in the trade in enslaved people. Try to find out about companies, people or buildings that are associated with the trade in your chosen city. Make notes of your findings and present these to the rest of the class. You might choose to present your findings as a poster or digital presentation.

5 Choose one of the smaller ports that were involved in the slave trade. You can either choose one of the ports mentioned in this chapter, or another one of interest to you. Research the role of your chosen port in the slave trade. Present your findings to the rest of the class.

6 Use the information from this section to write a detailed paragraph that explains the reasons why the trade in enslaved people was important to British ports. You should aim to write an answer which includes several points. Write each point in a separate sentence.

1.3 The effects of the slave trade on African societies

You have seen how the arrival of Europeans on the African continent led to the establishment of the trade in goods and captive Africans. From the seventeenth century onwards, as more and more labourers were demanded on the Caribbean plantations, the trade for goods such as cloth and ivory declined, and the trade in enslaved people became the dominant trade between Europe and Africa.

By the middle of the eighteenth century, almost every area of west and west-central Africa was affected by the slave trade.

The trade in enslaved people had a profound impact on African societies. In this section you will examine the following areas:

- loss of population
- impact on agriculture
- impact on African economies
- increase in war and conflict
- impact on culture and society

1.3.1 Loss of population

The trade in enslaved people had a devastating impact on Africa's population. During the period of the slave trade, more than 12 million people were transported across the Atlantic Ocean from Africa to the Americas. They did not return. This had a particular impact on west-central Africa.

In the eighteenth century alone, over 2 million captives were transported from west-central Africa into a life of slavery.

1.3.2 Impact on agriculture

As a result of the slave trade, large numbers of young men were lost, either killed in war or captured to be sold to traders. This meant that there were fewer young men to work on the land and produce food. In some places, women had to take on a greater share of the agricultural work due to the loss of men.

Food shortages

Villages and towns were often left deserted or were destroyed, and farm land or hunting areas were abandoned. This was either because there were not enough people left to farm them, or because they were too far away from the villages to be considered safe due to the fear of capture. Food shortages and famine became more frequent as a result.

Figure 1.10 Manioc, also known as cassava

Food was needed to feed the captives and crew on the Atlantic crossing. Farming in the region changed to prioritise the growth of crops that could be sold to provision the slave ships. This led to new methods of production and the introduction of crops such as **maize** and **manioc** (Figure 1.10), which were brought by Portuguese ships moving between Africa and the Americas.

1.3.3 Impact on African economies

Due to the slave trade, the trafficking of captives became the dominant trade between Europe and Africa. For example, north of the Congo River, Loango changed from being a major producer of cloth and an exporter of copper in the seventeenth century to become a major trader in captives during the eighteenth century.

The introduction of cheap foreign imports, brought over by traders, meant that the relative price of locally manufactured goods increased. Native crafts were often unable to compete with the cheaper European products.

In the longer term, the economies of the region became increasingly dependent on trade with Europe, and African societies became increasingly dependent on European economies.

1.3.4 Increase in war and conflict

Africans were not one population but many. African kingdoms fought wars against each other before the Europeans came to Africa. But the arrival of the Europeans encouraged conflict as money could be made from selling prisoners of war to traders. Traders formed alliances with African leaders and provided them with the weapons and means to attack rival African communities, in exchange for captives.

Dahomey

Dahomey was a kingdom in western Africa, in what is now southern Benin. It was originally a small coastal state, but by around 1750, it had become rich, partly as a result of its involvement in the slave trade. Dahomey obtained captives for sale through military raids and also through a complex trading system with African **middlemen**.

Ouidah

The town of Ouidah was a major slave-trading port. The section of the African coast on which Ouidah is situated was known as the 'Slave Coast'. Estimates suggest that over 1 million enslaved people passed through the port of Ouidah on their way to the '**New World**' (see Figure 1.11). Captives who were sold into slavery through Ouidah were mainly from neighbouring states raided by the Dahomian army. Others came from inland areas of Africa.

Figure 1.11 The Door of No Return in Ouidah, Benin. This is a memorial to the enslaved Africans who were taken from the slave port of Ouidah and transported across the Atlantic Ocean to a life of enslavement.

State of Ashanti

The state of Ashanti, which is located in modern-day Ghana, emerged at the end of the seventeenth century. Its power depended on the trade in enslaved people. In the 1770s the Ashanti kings provided over 1000 captives a year to European traders. Like the rulers of Dahomey, they waged war in order to obtain enslaved people to sell.

State of Kongo

By the seventeenth century, the state of Kongo, in west-central Africa, had become an intermediary in the slave trade. The state made money from taxing the passage of enslaved people through its territory.

Trade in weapons and munitions

The trade in guns from Europe in exchange for captives made it possible for African leaders to obtain more captives to sell. In the second half of the eighteenth century, the total number of guns exported from Europe to Africa was around 300,000 per year.

The historian James Walvin discusses the significance of guns:

Source 1.2

Guns gave strength to a state or a group (providing its neighbours did not also have them), and could tilt the balance of power in a region. It is even possible that guns persuaded some societies to become slave-traders; to protect themselves against neighbours, they needed guns. But guns could often only be acquired in return for slaves.

J. Walvin (2001) *Black Ivory: Slavery in the British Empire*

Gunpowder was also popular with African leaders. In the 1770s and 1780s more than a million pounds of gunpowder were imported to Africa from Britain. By 1790 this figure had increased to more than 2 million pounds.

 Note

The views of some historians have been included in this book in order to give you an idea of the range of different perspectives on this topic. You are not required to memorise the names and viewpoints of historians.

1.3.5 Impact on culture and society

The slave trade had a devastating impact on culture and society in west and west-central Africa.

This large region of Africa was home to kingdoms and city states, each with their own language, traditions and cultures. Africans were skilled in fields such as science, technology, medicine, astronomy and mathematics. They made decorative items in materials such as bronze, ivory, gold, brass, copper and terracotta (see Figure 1.12).

The kingdoms of Ife and Benin, in particular, were known for their bronze art. In some places, the removal of so many people as a result of the slave trade, as well as the introduction of European manufactured items, adversely affected African production.

The slave trade also affected how African people went about their daily lives. African communities that were at risk from the trade in enslaved people lived in fear of capture. Towers were built to protect settlements and the fear of kidnappings encouraged people to travel in groups.

Figure 1.12 Ivory salt cellar from Benin, dating from the sixteenth century

Olaudah Equiano describes his experience of watching for slave traders as a child:

Source 1.3

... when the grown people in the neighbourhood were gone far in the fields to labour, the children assembled together in some of the neighbours' premises to play; and commonly some of us used to get up a tree to look out for any assailant, or kidnapper, that might come upon us; for they sometimes took these opportunities of our parents' absence, to attack and carry off as many as they could seize.

Olaudah Equiano (1789) *The Interesting Narrative of the Life of Olaudah Equiano, or Gustavus Vassa, The African*

Equiano also describes the precautions taken by adults:

Source 1.4

... when our people go out to till their land, they only go in a body, but generally take their arms with them, for the fear of a surprise.

Olaudah Equiano (1789) *The Interesting Narrative of the Life of Olaudah Equiano, or Gustavus Vassa, The African*

How did Africans respond to the slave trade?

Africans responded to the threat posed by the slave trade in a variety of ways, including:

- constructing walled and fortified villages to defend against slave traders
- making use of mountains, caves and underground tunnels to escape
- planting poisonous and thorny trees and bushes for protection
- planting crops close to villages in coastal areas to make it safer for the people who tended them
- attacking 'slave factories' on the African coast
- attacking European ships
- trying to buy back the freedom of friends or relatives who had been taken as captives, if they were able to locate them. This was known as 'redemption'.

The historian Sylviane Diouf describes the practice of redemption:

Source 1.5

Far from abandoning their relatives, African families who could, looked for them, pooled resources, walked to the slave ships, and tried to gain time and precious manpower by sometimes pawning a younger child in their place. Some offered themselves as substitutes, continued to promise money to the westerners long after the ships had left, and collected funds to free or repatriate their unknown, American-born grandchildren. They also engaged in the trading of other men, women and children as a means to protect their own from deportation.

S. A. Diouf (2004) *Fighting the Slave Trade: West African Strategies*

Key fact summary

The effects of the slave trade on African societies
The loss of large numbers of young African people had a negative impact on the population.
Farm land was often abandoned, either because it was unsafe or because there were not enough people to tend the land.
Native crafts were often unable to compete with cheap foreign imports.
African societies became increasingly dependent on European economies.
There was an increase in war and conflict as powerful states carried out raids to obtain captives for sale.
The introduction of guns encouraged war and conflict between states.
There was a disastrous impact on culture, agriculture and African economies.

Activities

7 Look at the list of words, phrases or names below. Read the information about the impact of the slave trade on African societies. Create a set of questions that can only be answered by the words or phrases in the list.

more than 12 million people	300,000
Ashanti	Dahomey
maize	Ouidah
middleman	gunpowder
Loango	redemption

8 a) Copy the table below. Use the information about the effects of the trade in enslaved people on African societies to complete the table. You should include relevant facts for each factor to show how it affected Africa.

Factor	Key points to show how it affected Africa
Loss of population	
Impact on agriculture	
Impact on African economies	
Increase in war and conflict	
Impact on culture and society	

b) Work with a partner. Decide which factor had the biggest impact on Africa. Be prepared to give reasons for your choice.

9 Make notes of all the ways in which African people defended themselves and their communities from the threat posed by the slave trade.

1.4 The effects of the slave trade on Caribbean plantations

Using this information in your assessment

You can use the information in this section to answer questions about 'The effects of the slave trade on West Indian plantations'. As explained earlier in this chapter, please note that use of the term 'West Indies' is outdated.

In 1492, Europeans made contact with the Americas. This led to the development of colonies in places such as Jamaica and Barbados in the Caribbean, and Virginia in North America. In this topic we will focus on the Caribbean, which has also been known historically as the 'West Indies'.

Why is the Caribbean sometimes referred to as the West Indies?

The Caribbean includes islands such as Cuba and Trinidad and mainland territories such as the Guianas and Belize in Central America. It was historically known as the West Indies because when the explorer Christopher Columbus first arrived there in 1492, he mistakenly believed that he had sailed to the 'Indies'. The 'Indies' meant east Asia and south-east Asia.

The territories of the Caribbean changed hands as the European powers competed for control in the region. By the seventeenth century, Britain had become the dominant power in the Caribbean, and British merchants and landowners made huge amounts of money from the exploitation of enslaved Africans.

1.4.1 Introduction of sugar

In the 1640s Dutch merchants introduced sugar to Barbados. It quickly became the dominant crop in the Caribbean. The result of this was that the previous system of small farms growing crops changed rapidly to one which was based on large plantations growing sugar cane. By 1774, a typical medium-sized plantation on British-owned Jamaica was 600 acres, with around 200 enslaved people who were forced to work there.

As sugar became more profitable, larger numbers of labourers were needed to grow, harvest and process the sugar cane. This meant that enslavers in the British colonies began to purchase ever more enslaved Africans. By 1800, almost 1 million Africans had been trafficked to Jamaica alone. Many of them were subsequently transported to territories elsewhere in the region.

1.4.2 Why were enslaved Africans used in the Caribbean?

When the Europeans first arrived in the Caribbean, they found that the hot and humid climate was very different from what they were used to. At first, they used the native peoples to work on the land. But large numbers died due to overwork and exposure to European diseases.

The Europeans also used **bond servants**. These were white Europeans who emigrated to the colonies for a fixed period of time. Some went voluntarily while others were sent as prisoners of war, political prisoners or convicts. Bond servants also found it difficult to adapt to the heat. As a result, the Europeans looked to Africa for slave labour. The advantage of slave labour, from the perspective of the European settlers, was that labourers did not need to be paid and therefore profits were higher. In addition, bond servants would be set free at the end of their period of servitude and might also be allocated a parcel of land. By contrast, enslaved people from Africa retained their enslaved status for life, as did their descendants.

Africans were regarded by the British and other Europeans as racially inferior, and this supposed inferiority was used as a justification for enslaving them.

In the eighteenth century, racist views of Africa were expressed by the Scottish philosopher David Hume:

Source 1.6

I am apt to suspect [Africans] to be naturally inferior to the whites. There scarcely ever was a civilised nation of that complexion, nor even any individual, eminent either in action or in speculation. No ingenious manufacture among them, no arts, no sciences.

D. Hume (1777) *Of National Characters* – revised version of an essay first published in 1748

The slave trade reinforced the racist attitudes that many British people held towards Africa and Africans. These views continued throughout the period of the Atlantic Slave Trade and beyond.

Caribbean islanders

Indigenous peoples inhabited the Caribbean islands before the arrival of the Europeans. These included the **Taino** of the Greater Antilles, and the **Kalinago** of the Lesser Antilles. Contact with the European settlers had a devastating impact on these populations.

You will learn more about the impact of the trade in enslaved people on the indigenous peoples of the Caribbean in Chapter 2.

Some of the effects of the slave trade on the Caribbean are shown below:

○ One significant impact of the slave trade on the Caribbean was the development of **Creole** languages. African languages merged with the languages of the European settlers – Spanish, Portuguese, Dutch, French and English – to become Creole languages. These languages were used not only by enslaved people, but also by the white settlers.

○ When the Europeans arrived in the Caribbean, they brought with them new crops, in addition to sugar. On Columbus' second voyage to the New World, he introduced plants such as oranges, lemons, pomegranates, figs and bananas, and brought various seeds and cuttings of crops such as wheat, chickpeas, radishes and onions.

○ Slave-trade voyages also introduced to the Caribbean crops and foodstuffs that had been purchased to feed the captives and crew during the journey. These included the African kola nut, which could be used to improve the taste of water that had been stored in wooden casks for a long time on the voyage across the Atlantic. Other west African foodstuffs that made their way to the New World included plantains, rice, yams and millet.

Ultimately, the slave trade had a disastrous impact on the Caribbean territories. You will explore this further in Chapter 2.

Key fact summary

The effects of the slave trade on Caribbean plantations
By the seventeenth century, Britain was the dominant power in the Caribbean.
Sugar was introduced into the Caribbean in the 1640s, which led to the establishment of plantations on the islands.
Europeans initially used native people and bond servants to work on the land but turned to Africa to obtain slave labour.
By 1800, almost 1 million Africans had been trafficked to Jamaica alone.
Creole languages developed in the Caribbean as African languages merged with those of the European settlers.
New crops and foodstuffs were brought to the Caribbean as a result of the trade in enslaved people.
In the long term, the slave trade had a disastrous impact on the Caribbean islands.

Activity

10 Create a mind map or spider diagram to summarise what you have learned in this section about the effects of the slave trade on the Caribbean.

You might choose to do the planning for this task in pairs or small groups, but it would be a good idea to complete the mind map on your own in your workbook or work file. This will give you a learning check on how well you know the information.

1.5 'Slave factories' on the African coast

'Slave factories' or 'slave castles' were camps or forts built on the west coast of Africa by the Europeans. Their purpose was to hold captives until they could be sold and placed on board ships. At the height of the slave trade, there were more than 60 slave castles on a stretch of coast less than 300 miles long. Today, the remains of around 30 constructions can still be seen.

One of the best-known slave castles is Elmina Castle in modern-day Ghana, which was built in 1482 by the Portuguese and operated by the Dutch from 1637 (Figure 1.13).

Figure 1.13 Elmina Castle

A few miles away is Cape Coast Castle, which was built in the 1650s by Sweden but owned by the British from the 1660s (Figure 1.14). Both of these slave castles were in use during the period you are studying.

Figure 1.14 Cape Coast Castle

The historian Hugh Thomas describes Cape Coast Castle, as it was redeveloped by the English, after its capture in 1664:

Source 1.7

The new fortification consisted of outworks, platforms, and bastions; with apartments for the governor-in-chief, the director-general, the factors, clerks, and mechanics, as well as the soldiers. There were magazines, warehouses, storehouses, granaries, guard rooms, and two large water tanks, or cisterns, built of English brick and local mortar. 'Slaveholds' were established to confine 1,000-1,500 captives.

H. Thomas (1997) *The Slave Trade: The History of the Atlantic Slave Trade 1440–1870*

1.5.1 Conditions in the slave castles

Cape Coast Castle employed a chief agent, warehouse keeper and bookkeeper, in addition to a chaplain and **surgeon**. There were also blacksmiths and carpenters, and a 100-strong military garrison. 'Castle slaves' were enslaved people who were forced to work as porters, cooks, washerwomen and labourers.

Treatment of captives in the slave castles

Captives were often brought to the slave factories by local African chiefs or rulers. Upon arrival, they were examined by a surgeon. Those who were judged to be fit were bought and **branded** on the chest with a hot iron. This was intended to stop the African traders from switching bought captives for 'unfit' ones.

> CAUTION: SENSITIVE CONTENT

At Bunce Island, on the Sierra Leone River, captives were branded on the chest with the initials RAC to represent the Royal African Company, or with the letters DY to represent the Duke of York. Male captives were in greater demand than female captives because they attracted higher prices in the Americas.

Captives were kept in horrific conditions in the slave castles, sometimes for several months. They suffered both physical and psychological trauma during this time.

- Slave traders would cram more than 1000 people into dungeons that could barely hold 200.
- Men were separated from women.
- There was a lack of ventilation – windows were small openings cut into the prison walls.
- There was no **sanitation**, and the floors of the dungeons were covered in the excrement and vomit of the captives.
- Food was often scarce.
- Disease spread rapidly, and outbreaks of **malaria** and **yellow fever** were common.
- People who tried to resist would be shut in a dungeon named the 'condemned cell' where they would be left to die.
- Women faced sexual abuse. English officers at Cape Coast Castle would select women from among the captives and those who resisted being raped by the officers were thrown into punishment cells. At Bunce Island, historians have noted among the ruins the existence of a chamber in the women's holding yard that they have called the 'rape house', where, they believe, female captives were taken to be sexually abused.

At the seaboard side of the slave castles was the 'Door of No Return'. Those who survived conditions in the slave castles were taken outside through this portal to boats that were waiting for them. They were then transported to ships that would carry them across the Atlantic.

The experience of traders in the slave castles

In contrast to the conditions experienced by the captives in the slave factories, the European traders lived in luxury. Bunce Island had a golf course served by caddies who wore loincloths made of tartan wool that was imported from Glasgow. The living quarters for the traders at Bunce Island also had a fake fireplace to make them feel more at home and there was an ice store, which allowed them to chill their drinks. There was also a graveyard – nearly half of the white population of the island died each year, from a combination of drink and tropical diseases.

Key fact summary

'Slave factories' on the African coast
Slave factories or slave castles were used to hold captives until they could be sold.
Captives were kept in overcrowded and unsanitary conditions in poorly ventilated dungeons.
Diseases spread in the cramped conditions.
Food shortages were common.
Captives would be examined by surgeons before being bought and branded.
Women suffered sexual abuse.
Anyone who attempted to resist would be severely punished.

Activities

11 Read the information in this section about slave factories on the African coast. Answer the following questions:

  a) What were slave factories?

  b) What was the purpose of slave factories?

  c) What happened to captives once they arrived at the slave factories?

  d) What were conditions like in the slave factories for the captive Africans? (You should aim to write a detailed answer to this question and include as much information as possible.)

  e) What was the 'Door of No Return'?

12 Choose one of the slave factories mentioned in this chapter:
  • Cape Coast Castle
  • Elmina Castle
  • Bunce Island.
  Research your chosen slave factory. Produce a leaflet that gives information about the history of the site and the conditions experienced by the people who were held captive there.

1.6 The economics and conditions of the 'Middle Passage'

The 'Middle Passage' was the second stage of the Triangular Trade. Captive Africans were transported across the Atlantic Ocean in the hold of ships that were originally designed for carrying goods.

In this section you will examine the:

○ economics of the Middle Passage
○ conditions of the Middle Passage
○ resistance on board slave ships.

1.6.1 The economics of the Middle Passage

The primary purpose of a slave-trading voyage was to make money. The economics of the slave trade required the maximum number of captives to be transported in the smallest possible space so that the voyage would make a large profit.

Captives would be transported in the hold of the ship, the area where cargo would usually be kept. On average, around 300 people were stored in the hold of slave ships, but this figure could vary.

The longer the voyage across the Atlantic, the more likely it was that captives would die.

○ The ship's captain could choose to pack as many captives into the hold as possible, knowing that a number would die. This was known as **tight pack**.
○ Alternatively, he could load fewer captives, giving them more space to lie down, in the hope that more would survive the voyage. This was known as **loose pack**.

Captains were keen to obtain the best prices for their captives upon arrival in the Caribbean. They were prepared to move from one island to another if prices were higher elsewhere or if demand was low.

Privilege slaves

Captains might also be given permission to transport so-called 'privilege slaves'. These were captives who could be sold by the captain for his own profit, over and above those he would be required to sell on behalf of the ship's owners.

Insurance for slave voyages

Slave voyages were risky for owners and investors. Journeys across the Atlantic could be affected by bad weather, poor navigation and resistance by the captives. These losses would result in a reduced profit at the end of the voyage. Insurance was therefore required for slave voyages. But insurance for slave ships did not cover deaths of captives from disease or sickness. This was because it was assumed that captives would die during the journey.

The importance of profit on the Middle Passage is illustrated by the case of the *Zong*.

What happened on the *Zong*?

The *Zong* was a slave ship owned by a Liverpool merchant.

- On 6 September 1781, the *Zong* left west Africa and sailed for Jamaica with 442 Africans on board.
- The voyage took longer than planned and a number of captives became ill.
- The captain faced a dilemma. Deaths of captives from disease on board the slave ships were not covered by insurance. However, if the captain could show that some of the captives were thrown overboard in order to save the rest of the 'cargo' or the crew, the insurers would cover the losses of the ship's owner.
- A decision was made to throw more than 130 sick Africans overboard and allow them to drown.
- A claim was made that a shortage of water forced the captain's hand to jettison the 'human cargo'. However, it was later revealed that it had rained for a day when some of the enslaved people were thrown overboard.
- When the *Zong* returned to Liverpool, the ship's owner made a claim of £30 for every person who was thrown overboard. But the insurers were suspicious and refused to pay.
- The case came to court in March 1783 and the insurers lost.
- The case was held purely as an insurance dispute, and nobody was ever prosecuted for the murders. Indeed, when the insurers appealed the original decision, the judge in the case stated his view that 'the case of slaves was the same as if horses had been thrown overboard'.

The case of the *Zong* inspired the artist J. M. W. Turner, whose painting *Slave Ship* is shown in Figure 1.15. It also inspired anti-slavery activists such as Granville Sharp, who tried, unsuccessfully, to have the crew of the *Zong* prosecuted. You will learn more about Sharp in Chapter 4.

Figure 1.15 *Slave Ship* (1840) by the artist J. M. W. Turner. He based the painting partly on an eighteenth-century poem that described a slave ship caught in a typhoon, and partly on the case of the *Zong*

1.6.2 The conditions of the Middle Passage

It is estimated that as many as 2 million Africans died during the Atlantic crossing. Conditions on board the slave ships were appalling:

CAUTION: SENSITIVE CONTENT

○ Men would be chained together in the ship's hold. Some captives might have to spend several weeks or even months there before the ship set sail from the coast of Africa.
○ The captives would be forced to lie flat on wooden planks with no space to turn around. The movement of the ship would cause painful sores as the wooden planks rubbed against their skin.
○ There was little sanitation, apart from waste buckets that were often overflowing. This meant that people were forced to lie in their own waste and vomit.
○ There was no air, and it was unbearably hot and smelly. It was said that sailors could smell an approaching slave ship from five miles away.
○ The cramped and filthy conditions allowed illness to spread. Already weakened by the journey, captives were more susceptible to the spread of disease. Many captives died from **dysentery**, known at the time as 'the bloody flux', and **smallpox**. Those who became ill or died were thrown overboard.
○ The captives were fed twice a day and those who refused to eat were force fed.
○ A limited amount of water was provided but this was not enough to counter the effects of dehydration.
○ The captives were taken up on deck once or twice per day and were forced to dance for exercise. This was also a form of humiliation.
○ Women and children were kept separate from the men and were usually left unchained.
○ Sexual abuse of the female captives by the ship's male crew was common.

Cruelty towards captives

Captives faced cruelty from the crew and could be whipped or beaten if they showed any signs of resistance. One specific example of cruelty on board a slave ship was highlighted in Parliament in 1792 by the MP William Wilberforce, a prominent opponent of the slave trade. Wilberforce spoke of how Captain John Kimber of the slave ship *Recovery* had whipped a fifteen-year-old African girl to death. Kimber was later put on trial for murder but was found not guilty.

It is difficult for us to imagine the full horror of the Middle Passage. First-hand accounts can give us an insight into the experience of the captives. Three such accounts are given below.

Olaudah Equiano was transported from Africa to the Caribbean as a child. He describes conditions in the ship's hold during his own journey across the Atlantic:

Source 1.8

The closeness of the place, and the heat of the climate, added to the number in the ship, being so crowded that each had scarcely room to turn himself, almost suffocated us. This produced copious perspirations, so that the air soon became unfit for respiration, from a variety of loathsome smells, and brought on a sickness among the slaves, of which many died … This deplorable situation was again aggravated by the galling of the chains, now become insupportable; and the filth of the necessary tubs, into which the children often fell, and were almost suffocated. The shrieks of the women, and the groans of the dying, rendered it a scene of horror almost inconceivable.

Olaudah Equiano (1789) *The Interesting Narrative of the Life of Olaudah Equiano, or Gustavus Vassa, The African*

Thomas Clarkson, an anti-slavery activist who gathered evidence of conditions on the Middle Passage, spoke to a witness who had worked as a member of the crew on a slave ship. The witness described conditions in the hold, highlighting the lack of air:

Source 1.9

The misery which the slaves endure in consequence of too close a stowage is not easily to be described. I have heard them frequently complaining of heat, and have seen them fainting, almost dying for want of water.

T. Clarkson (1789) *An Essay on the Comparative Efficiency of Regulation or Abolition, as Applied to the Slave Trade*

Alexander Falconbridge, a surgeon on board a slave ship who later became an opponent of the trade in enslaved people, describes the food that was given to the captives:

Source 1.10

The diet ... while on board, consists chiefly of horse-beans, boiled to the consistence of a pulp; of boiled yams and rice, and sometimes a small quantity of beef or pork. The latter are frequently taken from the provisions laid in for the sailors. They sometimes make use of a sauce, comprised of palm-oil, mixed with flour, water and pepper, which the sailors call *slabber-sauce*.

A. Falconbridge (1790) *An Account of the Slave Trade, on the Coast of Africa*

Deaths of crew members were common on board slave ships. Large numbers of sailors also died of disease on the African coast. The suffering of the white crews of slave ships was later highlighted by opponents of the slave trade, who believed that it would attract the sympathy of the public and help their cause.

1.6.3 Resistance on board slave ships

Resistance on board slave ships was common, but mostly unsuccessful. Historians have calculated that there was a revolt on a British slave ship once every two years. John Newton, a former slave-ship captain who later became an anti-slavery activist, said of resistance on the slave ships: 'It is always taken for granted, that [the captives] will attempt to gain their liberty if possible.'

Acts of resistance ranged from minor outbursts of violence to the complete overthrow of the crew and even capture of the ship itself. For example, in October 1786, a Dutch slave ship on the Gold Coast was seized by the captives. The ship was eventually destroyed by an explosion.

Figure 1.16 This drawing depicts some captive Africans in an act of resistance towards the crew of a slave ship

Uprisings were more common when the ship was still anchored and in sight of the African coast. During the voyage itself, mealtimes were regarded by the crew as the most likely time for an attempted uprising, with one crew member stating:

Source 1.11

[four o'clock in the afternoon is] the aptest time to mutiny [the slaves] being all on deck ... Therefore, all that time what of our men who are not employed in distributing victuals to them ... stand to their arms; and some with loaded matches at the great guns that yawn upon them, loaden with cartridge, till they have done ...

T. Phillips (1746) *Journal, Vol. VI, A Collection of Voyages and Travels*

The source below is taken from the logbook of the Liverpool slave ship *Unity*. It gives details of attempted uprisings by captives on board the ship.

Source 1.12

6 June 1770

The slaves made an insurrection which was soon quelled with the loss of two women.

23 June 1770

Died a girl slave, No. 13. The slaves attempted an insurrection, lost a man of Capt Monypenny's purchase, who jumped over board and was drown'd. Employed securing the men in chains and gave the women concerned 24 lashes each.

26 June 1770

The slaves this day proposed making an insurrection and a few of them got off their handcuffs but were detected in time.

27 June 1770

The slaves attempted to force up the gratings in the Night with a design to murder the whites or drown themselves, but were prevented by the watch. In the morning they confessed their intention and the women as well as the men were determined if disappointed of cutting of the whites, to jump overboard but in case of being prevented by their irons were resolved as their last resource to burn the ship. Their obstinacy put me under the Necessity of shooting the Ring Leader.

Liverpool Museums Archives Centre

Resistance by women and children

Women were able to play a role in revolts due to the fact that they were afforded relative freedom of movement on board the ships. This was also true of children. Women and children were kept in separate quarters, sometimes on deck. This allowed them to collect nails and other tools that could be used to unlock chains and manacles. For example, on the slave ship *Thomas*, bound for Barbados, female captives seized muskets, overpowered the crew and freed the male captives. They were unable to sail the ship back to Africa and it was eventually recaptured by a British warship.

Punishments

Brutal punishments were given to those who tried to resist. Ship captains would try to make an example of the ringleaders, to warn captives about the dangers of resistance and to discourage further revolt. Following one revolt on board the Danish ship, *Fredericus Quartus,* all of the ship's captives were forced to watch as the ringleader was executed.

Other forms of resistance

For some captives, suicide was also a form of resistance. While on deck, captives might try to jump overboard. The crews attempted to prevent this by rigging nets around the decks of the ships. Others refused to eat and would be force fed.

Olaudah Equiano witnessed suicide attempts and described these in his autobiography:

Source 1.13

One day, when we had a smooth sea and moderate wind, two of my wearied countrymen, who were chained together ... preferring death to such a life of misery, somehow made through the nettings and jumped into the sea: immediately another quite dejected fellow, who on account of his illness was suffered to be out of irons also followed their example; and I believe many more would very soon have done the same, if they had not been prevented by the ship's crew, who were instantly alarmed.

Olaudah Equiano (1789) *The Interesting Narrative of the Life of Olaudah Equiano, or Gustavus Vassa, The African*

Using this information in your assessment

Information about resistance on board slave ships could be used to answer a question about the experience of captives during the Middle Passage.

Key fact summary

The economics and conditions of the 'Middle Passage'
Captives would be transported across the Atlantic Ocean in the holds of ships – in either 'tight pack' or 'loose pack'.
Conditions on the Middle Passage were horrific and an estimated 2 million people died during the voyage.
Men were chained and forced to lie flat on wooden planks with no space to turn around.
The cramped, unsanitary conditions allowed diseases to spread.
Captives experienced brutal treatment at the hands of the crew.
Female captives suffered sexual abuse.
Attempts to resist during the Middle Passage were usually unsuccessful and ringleaders faced severe punishments, including execution.

Activities

13 Read the information and sources about the Middle Passage. Use the information to copy and complete the table below. Aim to include at least three facts for each aspect of the Middle Passage. For the heading 'Conditions experienced by captives on board the slave ships', try to include as much detail as possible.

Aspect of the Middle Passage	Key points
The difference between 'tight pack' and 'loose pack'	
Conditions experienced by captives on board the slave ships	
Treatment of captives by the crew	
The case of the *Zong*	
Resistance on board the slave ships	
The experience of captive women on board the slave ships	

14 Use the information from this section to write a report about the Middle Passage. You should ensure that you cover each of the aspects of the Middle Passage highlighted in the table above, and any other information that you find.

15 The sources below are about the Middle Passage. The authors of the sources have very different views about the conditions experienced by captives on board the slave ships. Read both sources and then answer questions a)–c).

Source A is adapted from a speech that was given in Parliament by an MP who was trying to defend slavery. He presents false claims about the Middle Passage in an attempt to make conditions seem favourable.

Source A

The slaves' quarters on board ship are fitted up as well as possible ... They have several meals a day, some of their own country provisions with the best sauces of African cookery; and, by way of variety, another meal of pulse, a porridge after the European taste. After breakfast they have water to wash themselves, while their quarters are perfumed with spices and lime juice. Before dinner they are entertained with singing and dancing in the manner of their country.

→

Source B is from the reply to this speech by the MP William Wilberforce, who was an opponent of slavery. He presents a more accurate picture of the Middle Passage.

Source B

One slave captain has told me that he never leaves the coast of Africa during daylight, because the slaves are so upset ... They get so little food and water that even the Assembly of the planters in Jamaica suggested that Parliament act to improve it. Some may talk of perfumes and lime juice, but ... Sir George Young has testified that even in a ship which had spaces for another two hundred slaves, the stench was intolerable. The truth about the song and dance is that, for the sake of exercise, those miserable creatures ... are forced to dance by the terror of the lash.

a) Read **Source A** carefully. Based on what you have learned about the Middle Passage, explain why the speech by the pro-slavery MP is inaccurate. (Hint: select words or phrases that demonstrate that he is attempting to make conditions on the Middle Passage seem favourable.)

b) Read **Source B** carefully. Based on what you have learned about the Middle Passage, explain why the speech by William Wilberforce is accurate. (Hint: select words or phrases that match what you have learned in this section about conditions on the Middle Passage.)

c) Read **Sources A and B** again carefully. Select points from each source that show that the sources *disagree* with one another about the conditions experienced by captives on board the slave ships. Copy and complete the table below.

Points from Source A about conditions experienced by captives on board the slave ships	Points from Source B about conditions experienced by captives on board the slave ships that disagree with Source A

Summary

The Triangular Trade had a profound impact on Britain, Africa and the Caribbean. At each stage of the triangle, Europeans made a profit and Africans were exploited.

British ports such as London, Bristol and Liverpool profited financially from involvement in the trade in enslaved people and many jobs were created as a result.

The slave trade had a devastating impact on society and culture in Africa. It also had a negative impact on agriculture and the African economies. The introduction of guns encouraged conflict between states as money could be made from selling captive people to traders.

The introduction of sugar and the subsequent development of plantations had a significant, and ultimately destructive, impact on the Caribbean.

Enslaved people faced horrific conditions in the slave factories on the African coast, and on the ships that carried them across the Atlantic Ocean. The overriding consideration was the desire to make money and little consideration was given to the suffering of the enslaved African people.

Activity

16 Create a set of revision notes for this chapter. You should ensure that your notes cover the following headings:
- The organisation and nature of the slave trade
- The effects of the slave trade on British ports
- The effects of the slave trade on African societies
- The effects of the slave trade on Caribbean plantations
- Slave factories on the African coast
- The economics and conditions of the Middle Passage.

Glossary

Term	Meaning
Auction	A public sale in which goods or property are sold to the highest bidder.
Bond servants	Also known as indentured servants. Men and women who agreed to work for a set number of years; after this period of time they would become free.
Branding	Burning a mark into the skin of a person to show 'ownership'.
Coffle	A line of enslaved people, chained and driven along together.
Colonies	Countries under the control of another country.
Copper sheathing	Copper plates that were fixed to the underwater hull of a ship.
Creole	Creole languages are languages that developed from the merging of African languages with the languages of European settlers in the Caribbean.
Dysentery	An infection affecting the intestines causing severe diarrhoea.
Kalinago	An indigenous people of the Lesser Antilles of the Caribbean.
Loose pack	Loading fewer captives into the hold of a ship and giving them more space to lie down, in the hope that more would survive the voyage.
Maize	Another word for corn.
Malaria	A deadly disease passed on by mosquito bites.
Manioc	A tropical plant with branches and long roots that can be eaten. Also known as cassava.
Middlemen	People or companies that buy things from the people who produce them and sell them to the people who want to buy them.
Middle Passage	The journey from west Africa to the Caribbean; the second stage in the Triangular Trade.
New World	The areas of the Americas that Europeans believed they 'discovered' in the fifteenth century.
Plantations	Estates where crops such as sugar, tobacco and coffee were grown.

→

Term	Meaning
Royal Charter	A formal document signed by a monarch that gives an organisation particular rights.
Sanitation	Having access to clean water and facilities such as toilets.
Scramble	A type of sale in which the captives were kept together in an enclosure. Buyers paid a fixed sum in advance and, on a signal, rushed in and grabbed the captives they wanted.
Smallpox	A serious contagious disease caused by a virus.
Surgeon	Those who were employed as surgeons often lacked medical knowledge. They received 'head money' paid for healthy arrivals. Surgeons examined the captives on the African coast and inspected the captives daily during the voyage.
Taino	A member of an indigenous people of the Greater Antilles and the Bahamas.
Tight pack	Packing as many captives into the hold of a ship as possible.
Yellow fever	A tropical disease spread by a virus affecting the liver and kidneys.
Yoke	A wooden bar or frame by which two animals (or, in this case, people) are joined together at the neck.

Chapter 2

Britain and the Caribbean

The aim of this chapter is to examine the impact of the Atlantic Slave Trade on Britain and the Caribbean.

It will outline the importance of the tropical crops that were grown in the colonies, with a focus on sugar. It will discuss the influence of the British in the Caribbean and the impact of the trade in enslaved people on the British economy. This will include a study of industries such as shipbuilding, banking and textiles, as well as other industries that benefited from access to trade with the Caribbean.

Finally, it will explore the disastrous impact of the trade in enslaved people on the development of the Caribbean islands.

Together, this will enable you to respond to questions from Key issue 2: Britain and the Caribbean.

Link to the assessment

National 4 and 5

Key issue 2: Britain and the Caribbean

- The importance of tropical crops such as sugar
- The influence of the British in the Caribbean
- The impact of the Caribbean trade on the British economy
- The negative impact of the slave trade on the development of the Caribbean islands

Background

Britain exploited the resources of the Caribbean and the forced labour of enslaved Africans to create vast wealth and build a powerful empire.

What do we mean by 'British colonies' in the Caribbean?

Technically speaking, prior to 1707, the 'British' colonies in the Caribbean were controlled by England. Scotland and England shared the same monarch from 1603, when King James VI of Scotland took over the English throne after the death of Queen Elizabeth I. But Scots did not have full trading privileges within the Empire until after the Act of Union of 1707, which created the United Kingdom of Great Britain. The Act of Union allowed Scottish merchants full access to the Caribbean territories.

Figure 2.1 A map showing the Caribbean islands and the European countries that claimed them during the period of the trade in enslaved people

England's conquests in the Caribbean began with Bermuda in 1609, and included St Kitts in 1623, Barbados in 1625 and Jamaica in 1655. Colonies were also established in Nevis, Antigua and Montserrat, while the Bahamas came under the direct control of the British crown in the eighteenth century. By the early nineteenth century, Britain had also taken control of Dominica, Saint Lucia, Saint Vincent, Tobago, Grenada and Trinidad. By 1800, the most profitable Caribbean colonies belonged to Britain. As the number and size of Britain's colonies grew, so too did the importance of the trade in enslaved people to the British economy.

Enslaved people were forced to work on the plantations of the Caribbean to produce goods that were in demand in Britain. These goods included sugar, coffee and cotton. Individuals made huge profits from ownership of plantations and from trade in goods that were produced in the Caribbean by enslaved people. The slave trade also created great wealth for Britain as industries such as shipbuilding boomed.

The presence of the British in the Caribbean had a negative impact on the development of the Caribbean islands. The legacy of the exploitation of the Caribbean can still be seen today, both in the physical remains of slavery and in the economic and social problems that exist in Caribbean societies.

Edward Colston

One example of a British merchant who became rich as a result of the slave trade is Edward Colston (Figure 2.2). Colston was born in Bristol in 1636. In 1680 he joined the Royal African Company and served on its board for 12 years. During this time the Royal African Company transported over 84,000 captive Africans to the Americas and the Caribbean. It is estimated that more than 18,000 Africans died during the journey. Colston made a fortune from his involvement in the Royal African Company. He later donated money to several charitable causes in Bristol and London, including schools and hospitals.

Figure 2.2 Statue of Edward Colston being thrown into the River Avon in Bristol

In 1895, a statue of Colston was erected in Bristol's city centre as a memorial to his charitable works. For many years, local groups campaigned for the removal of the Colston statue. The campaign came to a head on 7 June 2020, when anti-racism protestors brought down the statue, dragged it through the streets and threw it into the River Avon. In January 2022, four people accused of illegally removing the statue were cleared of criminal damage.

In the wake of the toppling of the Colston statue, a number of British companies issued an apology for their historic links to slavery or the slave trade. These included the pub chain, Greene King, and the insurance market, Lloyd's of London. You will learn more about Lloyd's of London later in this chapter.

Using this information in your assessment

Colston died in 1721, which is several decades before the period covered in our topic. Therefore, information about Colston cannot be used to gain credit for questions that ask about the impact of the slave trade on Britain. However, his story is of interest as background to this chapter because it illustrates for us not only the great wealth that individuals could amass through involvement in the trading of enslaved people, but also the ways in which British towns and cities benefited financially from investments and donations made by these individuals.

Lasting ties and influence

The influence of the British in the Caribbean continued long after the end of the slave trade in 1807 and the abolition of slavery itself in 1833. The 'British West Indies' remained an important part of the **British Empire** and trade with the Caribbean helped Britain maintain its position as a dominant world power. There was also a period of significant emigration from the Caribbean to Britain, particularly in the immediate decades after the Second World War.

In the second half of the twentieth century, many of Britain's colonies in the Caribbean gained their independence, but maintained a connection with Britain through membership of the **Commonwealth** and retention of the British monarch as Head of State.

In recent years, some of Britain's former colonies have sought to cut ties with the British crown. One example is Barbados, which became a republic in 2021, removing Queen Elizabeth II as Head of State, but choosing to remain within the Commonwealth. There have also been calls for compensation to be paid to the Caribbean by Britain and other European powers that controlled the former colonies.

When slavery ended in 1833, the former 'slave owners' received £20 million in compensation, a sum equivalent to 40 per cent of the Treasury's annual income at that time. The bill was so vast that it was not paid off until 2015. But the enslaved people themselves received nothing. In fact, they were tied to another form of unfree labour as 'apprentices' for fixed terms until finally obtaining their freedom in 1838.

2.1 The importance of tropical crops such as sugar

Britain's deep involvement in the slave trade and its colonisation of the Caribbean islands meant that products such as cotton, coffee and sugar went from being luxury imports that only the wealthy could afford to cheaper produce that ordinary people could also access. As a result of the popularity of these products, ordinary people became just as dependent on the slave trade as merchants and enslavers.

Sugar was the most important of the tropical crops. In fact, in the period between the middle of the seventeenth century and the middle of the nineteenth century, sugar became the most important commodity in the world.

2.1.1 Sugar in the Caribbean

The sugar cane plant was introduced to the Caribbean during the seventeenth century (Figure 2.3). Sugar grew well in the climate of the Caribbean islands, and it quickly became the main crop produced on the plantations. Overall, nearly 70 per cent of all enslaved Africans in the Americas worked on plantations that grew sugar cane. In 1770, worldwide sugar production amounted to 200,000 tons, and 90 per cent was from the Caribbean.

Jamaica was a particularly lucrative sugar island. Between 1775 and 1824, half of the region's sugar came from Jamaica.

Figure 2.3 The sugar cane plant. Between 1766 and 1791, the British Caribbean produced over a million tons of sugar.

Sugar consumption

Sugar was originally a delicacy only available to the rich. But during the period of the slave trade, sugar became more widely available to ordinary people as standards of living began to improve. Between 1700 and 1709, the sugar consumption in Britain, per person, amounted to 4 pounds (weight). A century later this had risen to 18 pounds per person. Britain took around a third of all the sugar imported to Europe in the eighteenth century. From 1650 to 1800 there was a 2500 per cent increase in sugar consumption in Britain.

Other uses of sugar

One of the by-products of processing sugar cane was **molasses**. This was **fermented** and **distilled** to produce rum. Rum was a staple on slave ships and the ships of the Royal Navy, and was often used as part payment for the crews. Sugar was also used in puddings and jam and as a preservative in addition to salt.

2.1.2 Popularity of sugar

During the eighteenth century, sugar became increasingly popular as a sweetener in drinks such as tea and coffee. Coffee houses became fashionable in English towns and cities as places where people could go to meet, conduct business and exchange ideas (Figure 2.4). Towards the end of the eighteenth century, tea became more popular than coffee, especially after duties on tea were lowered in 1784. The demand for coffee and tea fuelled the demand for sugar, which, in turn, fuelled the demand for slave labour.

Figure 2.4 Drawing of the interior of a London coffee house, c.1690–1700. By 1740, London alone had 550 coffee houses.

The result of this was wealth on a scale that is hard for us to imagine. In 1773, for example, the value of British imports from the small sugar island of Grenada was five times higher than the value of imports from the thirteen American colonies. Historian Adam Hochschild describes the sugar islands of the Caribbean in the following terms:

Source 2.1

Think of them as the Middle East of the late eighteenth century. Just as oil drives the geopolitics of our own time, the most important commodity on European minds then was sugar, and the overseas territories that mattered most were the islands so wonderfully suited for growing it ... Over the course of the [eighteenth] century, some 60 per cent of all slaves brought anywhere in the Americas were taken to the relatively small area of the Caribbean. Sugar was king.

A. Hochschild (2005) *Bury the Chains: The British Struggle to Abolish Slavery*

2.1.3 Beyond sugar

Sugar was not the only crop grown in the colonies. The Caribbean plantations provided cotton for the factories of the early **Industrial Revolution.** By 1800, Demerara and Berbice were the leading producers of both cotton and coffee. Indigo and rice also grew well in the climate of the colonies.

Tobacco was the first major export crop in the Caribbean, but it was unable to compete with tobacco that was produced in the British colony of Virginia in North America. Early settlers in

Virginia had tried to farm sugar, but without success. They found, however, that tobacco grew well in the climate and soil of the region. From the 1620s onwards, tobacco became the region's major export.

Merchants in Glasgow made money from tobacco grown by enslaved people in North America. The Merchant City area of Glasgow city centre was home to the 'tobacco barons' who made their money from the tobacco trade. One of the largest tobacco firms was that of John Glassford and Co. Another prominent tobacco lord was Andrew Buchanan. Both Glassford and Buchanan have streets named after them in Glasgow's city centre.

Using this information in your assessment

Information about Glasgow and the tobacco trade could be used to answer questions that ask about the 'impact of the slave trade on the British economy'.

William Cunninghame

The Gallery of Modern Art in Glasgow, originally the Cunninghame Mansion, was built in 1778 as the house of William Cunninghame, one of Glasgow's most prominent eighteenth-century merchants (Figure 2.5). Cunninghame had interests in both the Caribbean sugar trade and the tobacco trade with Virginia. He owned the Grandvale sugar plantation in Westmoreland, Jamaica, which had an enslaved workforce of 300 people.

Figure 2.5 The Gallery of Modern Art in Glasgow, originally the Cunninghame Mansion

Key fact summary

The importance of tropical crops such as sugar
Sugar became more widely available to ordinary people during the period of the slave trade as standards of living rose.
Sugar was popular as a sweetener in drinks such as coffee and, later, tea.
The demand for sugar fuelled the demand for slave labour on the Caribbean islands.
Sugar was the most important of the tropical crops.
Other crops such as cotton, coffee, indigo and rice were grown in the colonies.
Ordinary people became reliant on the trade in enslaved people for access to the consumer goods produced on the plantations.
Merchants in Glasgow made money from involvement in the tobacco trade.

Activities

1 Read the information in this section. Write a report about the importance of sugar in the period 1770–1807. You should include the following information:
   - Reasons why sugar became so popular in the period you are studying.
   - Uses of sugar in the period you are studying.
   - Information and statistics to illustrate the importance of sugar in the Caribbean.
   - Information and statistics to illustrate the importance of sugar to the British economy.

2 Choose one of the other tropical crops that were grown in the Caribbean. Try to find out more about this crop and its importance to the British economy.

2.2 The influence of the British in the Caribbean

Britain's colonies in the Caribbean were part of a wider empire that, until the American Revolution of 1775–83, also included territory in what became the United States of America.

2.2.1 Management of the colonies

During the period of British rule in the Caribbean, the colonies were managed by Governors. For example, Sir Archibald Campbell, a Scottish landowner, was appointed Governor of Jamaica in 1781. The Governors lived in vast mansions, built in the British style, many of which are still in use today as government buildings. Government House in the Bahamas was built between 1803 and 1806 and is the official residence of the **Governor-General** of the Bahamas today (Figure 2.6).

Figure 2.6 Government House, the Bahamas. Note the statue of Christopher Columbus on the steps.

British society in the colonies

The British established societies in the colonies. For example, they built towns such as Kingston in Jamaica, which had a population of around 26,000 people in 1788. This was roughly 10 per cent of the overall population of the island. The white residents of Kingston had access to markets, taverns, coffee houses and a circulating library. They could also visit the theatre. Jamaica had a legislative assembly that was responsible for making local laws and raising local taxes. There was a **militia**, in which all white men between the ages of 16 and 60 were required to serve. White men also participated in local courts as jurors or as **magistrates**.

One major result of the presence of the British and other European settlers in the Caribbean was the emergence of a group of people who were born as a result of the sexual exploitation of black women by white enslavers, the so-called 'coloured' population. By the end of slavery in the British Caribbean, Jamaica had 16,000 white people, 310,000 enslaved people and 31,000 people who were referred to as 'coloured'. '**Free people of colour**' or '**free**

> **Note**
>
> The term 'coloured' is outdated and has long been regarded as offensive. Today, we would use the term 'mixed heritage'.

coloureds' were terms used to describe people of African or African–European descent who were not enslaved. They had either been born free or had purchased or been granted their freedom. In Jamaica, 'free people of colour' were made to join the militia, but they were not allowed to serve as officers. They did not have the right to vote, and could not hold public office or serve as jurors or magistrates.

There are numerous towns in the Caribbean that are named after places in Britain, for example, Aberdeen in Jamaica, Brighton in Barbados and Montrose in Tobago. Georgian-style architecture from the period of the slave trade can be found in Caribbean towns such as the port of Falmouth in Jamaica (Figure 2.7).

Figure 2.7 The court house in Falmouth, Jamaica, built in the Georgian style that was popular in Britain in the eighteenth century

2.2.2 Homes built for enslavers

Some enslavers chose to live in Britain, leaving the day-to-day running of their plantations to **overseers** or managers. Those who chose to live in the Caribbean built lavish homes on their plantations. One example is Rose Hall **Great House** in Jamaica, which was built between 1778 and 1790 by John Palmer, a wealthy British enslaver (Figure 2.8). At its peak, the plantation covered over 6500 acres and more than 2000 enslaved people were forced to labour there under degrading conditions. Rose Hall Great House was restored in the 1960s and is now a tourist attraction.

The Great Houses became the focal point of island life for the white settlers. Enslavers entertained local white society with balls and parties.

Figure 2.8 Rose Hall Great House, in Montego Bay, Jamaica

2.2.3 Profiting from plantations and enslaved people

Individuals emigrated from Britain to the colonies and made vast profits from ownership of Caribbean plantations and the forced labour of enslaved people. The London-based Scotsman, Sir Alexander Grant, had been a doctor in Jamaica. He eventually owned seven plantations in Jamaica, totalling 11,000 acres at his death in 1772, and was an enslaver to 672 men, women and children.

There were also a number of British institutions that made money from slave labour or ownership of plantations in the Caribbean. One such institution was the Church of England, which received funds from the Codrington Plantations on Barbados.

The legacy of the presence of the British in the Caribbean can also be seen in the physical remains of the plantations themselves. The Mona campus of the University of the West Indies in Jamaica is built on the site of two former sugar estates. The campus incorporates the remains of the Papine-Mona aqueduct, originally built in the 1750s to carry water from the Hope River to power the sugar mills of both estates (Figure 2.9). It also served a third sugar estate further north.

Figure 2.9 The Papine-Mona aqueduct

Key fact summary

The influence of the British in the Caribbean
Britain's colonies in the Caribbean were run on behalf of the British crown by Governors.
British settlers in the Caribbean maintained traditions from their home country.
Towns on the Caribbean islands were named after places in Britain.
Buildings in the Georgian architectural style demonstrate the influence of the British in the Caribbean.
Individual Britons could become wealthy through ownership of plantations on the islands.
Organisations such as the Church of England made money from slave labour on the plantations.
The presence of the British in the Caribbean led to the emergence of a community of people who were born as a result of the sexual exploitation of enslaved women by their enslavers.

Activities

3 Look at an atlas or map of the Caribbean islands. Try to identify places that are named after towns or locations in Britain. Share your findings with the rest of the class.

4 a) Information about individual British enslavers can be found in the 'Legacies of British slave-ownership' database, which is maintained by the Centre for the Study of the Legacies of British Slave-ownership at University College London (UCL). Use the search term 'Legacies of British slave-ownership' to find the database.

b) Use the database to research and identify individuals who made money from ownership of plantations in the Caribbean or who claimed ownership of enslaved Africans.

c) Present your findings as a report, poster or digital presentation.

2.3 The impact of the Caribbean trade on the British economy

You have learned that trade with the Caribbean supplied Britain with consumer goods such as sugar, rum, coffee and cotton. It also gave Britain a market for export goods, both in exchange for captive people in Africa, and to supply the plantations.

The slave trade had a significant impact on the British economy. In this section, you will examine the following areas:

- employment
- banking
- shipbuilding
- textiles
- growth of industries that supplied the plantations
- wealth and investment
- the overall importance of the slave trade to the British economy.

2.3.1 Employment

The trade in enslaved people created many jobs for British people, both in Britain and in the Caribbean. The Caribbean was an attractive destination for younger sons of landowners, who would not inherit the family estate and therefore had to make their fortune by other means. In the Caribbean, young, educated British men could work on the plantations as **bookkeepers** or overseers. They might also be employed as **attorneys** to handle the legal and financial affairs of plantations on behalf of enslavers who chose to live in Britain rather than the Caribbean. Sometimes they would oversee multiple estates at the same time. Doctors and lawyers were also in demand on the Caribbean islands.

The Scottish poet, Robert Burns, once intended to emigrate to Jamaica to work as a bookkeeper on a sugar plantation (Figure 2.10). His plans changed when his *Poems, Chiefly in the Scottish Dialect* was published by John Wilson of Kilmarnock in July 1786. The success of this publication meant that emigration was no longer such an attractive prospect and Burns decided to remain in Scotland.

Back in Britain, it was possible to find work on slave ships as crew or as a ship's surgeon. Other jobs associated with the trade in enslaved people included dock workers in the ports and carpenters

Figure 2.10 Robert Burns

or coopers (see page 76) on board slave ships. There were also jobs available in the industries that produced goods that could be shipped to Africa in exchange for captives, such as cloth, alcohol and pots and pans.

2.3.2 Banking

Annual returns from slave-trading voyages during the last half-century of British slavery averaged between 8 and 10 per cent, but merchants would not receive any of this money until after the voyage had been completed. In the meantime, they had to finance the voyage and pay for the ship and the crew. Finance came in the form of **bills of credit**. Ships were financed by a group of investors who met at places like the Jamaica Coffee House in London (Figure 2.11).

Figure 2.11 Plaque at the site of the Jamaica Coffee House (now the Jamaica Wine House) in London

Sailing across the Atlantic was dangerous. Voyages were at risk from storms, hurricanes and even piracy. This led to the establishment of insurance companies such as Lloyd's of London, which provided insurance for slave ships. Lloyd's of London was founded in 1688 in a London coffee house. By 1774, Lloyd's of London had grown in importance and had moved to a new building at the Royal Exchange in Cornhill.

Banks such as Barclays Bank began by investing in the slave trade. The Bank of England made money available for slave ship voyages and the City of London became the financial centre of the slave trade.

2.3.3 Shipbuilding

From the late seventeenth century onwards, a major shipbuilding industry developed around Liverpool.

The growth of shipbuilding led to the creation of jobs in building, fitting and repairing the ships. There were also jobs available for sail makers, rope makers and joiners. Slave ships required chains and manacles for the captives, which created jobs for metal workers.

Wales made money from **copper smelting** to produce the copper sheathing for the bottom of slave ships. In 1690, Wales didn't contribute to the global output of smelted copper, which amounted to 2400 tons. By 1800, production of smelted copper worldwide was 17,200 tons and over 40 per cent of this was smelted in Wales.

2.3.4 Textiles

The trade in enslaved people provided British industries with the raw materials that were turned into manufactured goods in Britain and then sold for huge profits in Europe and in the colonies.

Raw cotton from the plantations was imported from the Americas to be transformed into cloth. Some of this cloth was sold in Britain, while some was sold in Africa in exchange for captives.

Prior to the start of the eighteenth century, the main market for Britain's exports of woollen textiles was Europe. Involvement in the slave trade opened up access to markets further afield, including Africa and the colonies. Cloth manufacturers in Lancashire and Yorkshire could sell their goods easily through the port of Liverpool. After 1778, cotton grown by enslaved people became the main raw material for the Scottish textile industry, and Jamaica was the most significant export market. In Devon, locally produced cloth was exported to Africa and the Americas. Welsh fabric, a woollen fabric known as 'Welsh cotton' or 'Welsh plains', was exported to the Caribbean to provide clothing for enslaved people.

2.3.5 Growth of industries that supplied the plantations

There was also a demand for goods produced in Britain to supply the Caribbean territories. This benefited many industries, such as those shown below:

- Scottish herring was sent to the Caribbean plantations as food for enslaved people.
- South-west Ireland exported beef, butter and other salted provisions.
- Birmingham produced brass pots, kettles and pans.
- Wales sent copper to the plantations to make the copper vessels used in the making of sugar and distilling of rum.
- In Cornwall, merchants from Falmouth specialised in the luxury trade in silks and wines to the Caribbean and American plantations.
- Glass produced in Bristol was used to transport brandy and rum processed in the city.

There were also goods produced to supply enslavers and their families, for example, candles, books and furniture.

2.3.6 Wealth and investment

The trade in enslaved people created great wealth for Britain. The average annual value of goods exported from Britain to the Caribbean by the 1770s exceeded £1.33 million. The British government also made money from taxes associated with the slave trade.

Individuals and families made fortunes from trading enslaved people. As a result of these fortunes, families could move from the middle class to the aristocracy and landowning classes, often by marriage.

Many stately homes built between the 1660s and 1820s have links to money from the slave trade. One example is Auchincruive House, in Ayrshire, Scotland (Figure 2.12). Auchincruive House was built in 1767 by merchant and slave trader Richard Oswald. Oswald was the principal owner of Bunce Island slave castle, which you learned about in Chapter 1.

Figure 2.12 Auchincruive House, Ayrshire

Across Britain, money from the trade in enslaved people was used to finance the construction of public buildings such as churches, village halls and schools. For example, Dollar Academy in Clackmannanshire (Figure 2.13) was founded using money left in the will of the slave trader John McNabb. The Trans-Atlantic Slave Trade Database shows four slave voyages for McNabb from London between 1789 and 1791.

Figure 2.13 Dollar Academy, Clackmannanshire

Profits from the slave trade were invested in British industry. Wealthy merchants invested in industries such as coal and iron. Money from the trade in enslaved people was used to build canals and railways across Britain. Enslavers also helped to finance the steam engine of James Watt.

Legacies of the slave trade

The amount of wealth that was created by the slave trade, along with the role it played in shaping British history, was revealed by University College London's *Legacies of British Slave-ownership* project. Among other things, the project showed that 10–20 per cent of Britain's wealthy citizens had **significant** links to slavery.

When slavery was ended in the British Empire, vast sums were paid in compensation to around 46,000 former enslavers. This money was typically reinvested in British industry. For example, the Glasgow, Paisley, Kilmarnock and Ayr Railway Company received investment from former enslavers.

The benefits of the reinvestment of compensation money extend to the present day. Nothing was given to the former enslaved peoples, who did not gain their freedom until 1838.

2.3.7 How important was the slave trade to the British economy?

One of the key debates associated with the economic impact of the slave trade on Britain centres on the overall importance of the trade to the British economy – specifically the extent to which money from the trade in enslaved people financed the Industrial Revolution.

The historian Christer Petley provides a summary of historical interpretations of this issue:

Source 2.2

In *Capitalism and Slavery*, first published in 1944, Eric Williams (historian and first prime minister of Trinidad and Tobago) contended that slavery had contributed to the rise of Britain during the eighteenth century and had helped to fund the Industrial Revolution. But those arguments were heavily criticized by historians working during the final quarter of the twentieth century. Several scholars found that the profits of slavery contributed relatively little to direct investment in the sorts of industries that led Britain's nineteenth-century economic expansion ...

This has not, however, led to a wholesale dismissal of Williams' ideas ... Even some of those historians who do not see the slave colonies as a decisive factor in British industrialization concede that they provided huge markets for British manufactured goods and supplied the ever-cheaper plantation exports that drove a consumer revolution in European towns and cities.

C. Petley (2018) *White Fury: A Jamaican Slaveholder and the Age of Revolution*

As this chapter has demonstrated, the trade in enslaved people was clearly very important to the British economy. The table below summarises the key areas of economic impact.

Key fact summary

The impact of the Caribbean trade on the British economy
The slave trade created many jobs for British people, both in Britain and in the Caribbean.
Banks and insurance companies provided finance for slave-trade voyages.
Liverpool became a world leader in shipbuilding and many associated industries benefited as a result.
Textiles produced in Britain were exported to Africa and the Caribbean.
There was a demand for goods produced in Britain to supply the Caribbean islands.
Profits from the trade in enslaved people were invested in British industries.
Individuals and families became wealthy as a result of ownership of plantations.

Activities

5 a) Use the information in this chapter to create a mind map of all of the ways in which the trade in enslaved people had an impact on the British economy. You should include the following headings:

- Employment
- Banking
- Shipbuilding
- Textiles
- Growth of industries that supplied the plantations
- Wealth and investment
- Any other relevant factor.

b) Decide which of the factors had the biggest impact on the British economy. Rank the factors in order of importance, from most important to least important. Write a short paragraph justifying your selection.

6 The source below is from a letter written by a merchant to a London newspaper in April 1789. This was during the period when the slave trade was criticised. In the letter, the merchant expresses his views about the importance of the slave trade to the British economy.

Source C

Countrymen, think carefully about the benefits that the slave trade brings to this country. The manufacture of sugar, etc., could not be carried on, without the trade in enslaved Africans. Planters, merchants, and thousands of workers depend for their living on this trade with the West India Islands.

When researching any topic, historians need to make decisions about the reliability and usefulness of sources. They do this by asking the following questions about sources:

- Who wrote the source? For example, are they an eyewitness to events or a modern historian who is an expert in the topic?
- When was the source written? Is it primary or secondary?
- What type of source is it? For example, is it a newspaper, diary, letter, speech, textbook?
- Why was the source written? For example, was it written to persuade people to think a certain way?
- What does the source say about the topic? Is the information accurate, based on what you have learned?
- What important information has been missed out from the source? What key points have been missed out, based on your own knowledge?

a) Read **Source C** carefully.

→

b) Copy and complete the table. For each aspect of the source, explain whether this makes the source more or less useful to historians studying the impact of the trade in enslaved people on the British economy. The first box has been filled in for you.

Feature of the source	Answer	Comment about whether this makes the source more or less useful
Who wrote the source?	A merchant	He is an eyewitness to the impact of the slave trade on the British economy. He is likely to be very biased because he is making money from the trade in enslaved people.
When was the source written?		
What type of source is it?		
Why was the source written?		
What does the source say about the topic?		
What important information has been missed out?		

2.4 The negative impact of the slave trade on the development of the Caribbean islands

The Caribbean islands were the first place in the Americas to be conquered by the Europeans. The arrival of the Europeans had a devastating impact on the development of the region.

People had lived in the Caribbean for hundreds of generations before the coming of the Europeans. When the Europeans arrived, they found the Caribbean to be inhabited by diverse indigenous groups such as the Taino and the Kalinago. Nearly all of these indigenous groups were speakers of Arawakan languages. Scholars vary in their estimates of the total population of the Caribbean islands prior to the arrival of the Europeans, but most agree that the native Caribbean populations declined rapidly within a century. It is estimated that this decline could be as much as 90 per cent on some islands.

On islands like Cuba and Hispaniola, the local native population was almost completely wiped out by the white settlers. This happened either because of war, forced labour or contact with diseases such as smallpox, **typhus**, influenza, yellow fever and measles. This loss of population had a profound impact on language and culture in the Caribbean – around only a hundred Taino words are known to modern scholars.

Attempts at resistance

Indigenous people resisted and frequently attempted to fight back against the European settlers. For example, in their fight back against the Spanish, the Taino communities in Cuba, Jamaica, Puerto Rico and the Bahamas employed a variety of tactics including destroying crops, refusing to work and poisoning water supplies. The Kalinago, in particular, resisted the European colonisation of the Caribbean, especially during the period from the early seventeenth to the late eighteenth century.

The slave trade had a disastrous impact on the Caribbean. Its effects can be seen in the following areas:

- environmental impact
- economic impact.

2.4.1 Environmental impact

The slave trade had an environmental impact on the Caribbean as forests and lands were cleared to make way for sugar plantations. As sugar boomed, all available fertile land was converted to grow crops for export. In Barbados, for example, by 1767, 80 per cent of the island was planted in sugar cane – this was virtually all of the **arable** land in the colony. The reliance on sugar **monoculture** stripped the soil of nutrients within just a few harvests. Deforestation also made the Caribbean islands more vulnerable to drought, flooding and **erosion**.

The impact on wildlife was profound. Historians have estimated that, between 1600 and 1973, up to 50 species may have disappeared from the Caribbean, including 6 species of birds and 34 species of mammals. New species were introduced to the Caribbean as a result of contact with the Europeans. Columbus' second voyage brought attack dogs, horses, cattle, pigs, sheep, goats and chickens. There was also the accidental introduction of black rats, transported on slave ships, which fed on native plants and wildlife and spread diseases.

2.4.2 Economic impact

As small farms were replaced by sugar plantations, the Caribbean territories became over-reliant on sugar production. In Barbados, for example, sugar amounted to 93 per cent of the island's exports. But sugar crops were unpredictable. Good weather could lead to a bumper harvest, while drought could ruin the canes. There was also a risk of hurricanes, which destroyed crops.

Caribbean economies became over-dependent on long-distance trade – to export the sugar crop, but also to import supplies, including food. The focus on sugar cultivation meant that a limited amount of land was available for growing food. Imported food included corn from America, beans from England and saltfish from Newfoundland. There was a risk of delays in the shipping of food from Britain due to war or hurricanes.

The lasting legacy of slavery in the Caribbean

In the longer term, the slave trade resulted in the under-development of the Caribbean. Today, Caribbean societies face problems of poverty, illiteracy, inadequate public health facilities, poor quality housing and unequal access to education. The slave trade also created a highly racialised society on the Caribbean islands, which still persists today. In recent years, campaigners in the Caribbean have called for 'reparative justice', in the form of an apology from Britain for its role in slavery in the Caribbean and payment of reparations. This recognises the fact that compensation was paid to former enslavers when slavery ended in the British Empire, but the former enslaved people received nothing.

Key fact summary

The negative impact of the slave trade on the development of the Caribbean islands
The native populations of the islands were devastated by contact with the Europeans.
Forests and land were cleared to make way for sugar plantations.
The reliance on sugar stripped the soil of nutrients.
Deforestation left the Caribbean vulnerable to drought, flooding and erosion.
Indigenous wildlife became extinct.
The Caribbean islands became over-reliant on sugar production.
Caribbean economies became over-dependent on long-distance trade.

Activities

7 a) Work in pairs or in small groups. Take a large piece of paper and draw a triangle that fills most of the paper.

Your teacher will allocate a period of time. Fill the triangle with as many points as possible about the impact of the slave trade on the Caribbean. Once your time is up, leave your paper and move on to the next group's paper.

Your teacher will allocate another period of time. Add more information to the new group's paper outside the triangle. Keep moving round until all the information is on the paper or the paper is filled.

b) As a class, discuss and confirm that all points about the impact of the slave trade on the Caribbean have been included on the papers.

All of the class should take part in discussing and recording information.

8 Create a table of the reasons why the slave trade had a negative impact on the development of the Caribbean islands.

The table should list facts and clearly explained reasons. Find as many reasons as you can. An example is given below:

Reasons why the slave trade had a negative impact on the Caribbean islands	
Fact	**Reason**
Forests and lands were cleared to make way for sugar plantations.	This made the Caribbean islands more vulnerable to drought, flooding and soil erosion.

9 In this section you have learned a little about the impact of the arrival of the Europeans on the indigenous peoples of the Caribbean, specifically the Taino and the Kalinago. You may wish to do additional research to find out more. Be prepared to share your findings with the rest of the class.

Summary

Trade with the Caribbean was of huge importance to Britain. Individuals made vast profits and the British government benefited financially from taxes associated with the slave trade.

Britain came to rely on the consumer products that were produced in the Caribbean, in particular sugar.

Many jobs were created for British people, both in Britain and in the Caribbean. Industries such as shipbuilding, banking and textiles boomed.

Exploitation of the resources of the Caribbean created vast wealth for Britain but had a devastating impact on the population, economies, culture and landscape of the Caribbean territories.

Activities

10 a) Read the information about Britain's role in the trade in enslaved people. Prepare for a class debate on one or more of the following questions:
- 'Should all statues of enslavers be removed?'
- 'Should all buildings and streets that are named after enslavers be renamed?'
- 'Should Britain and other European countries pay compensation for their role in the slave trade?'

b) Make a list of arguments for and against your chosen question.

c) What is your own opinion? Write a paragraph to explain your view. Give reasons for your answer.

11 Create a set of revision notes for this chapter. You should ensure that your notes cover the following headings:
- The importance of tropical crops such as sugar
- The influence of the British in the Caribbean
- The impact of the Caribbean trade on the British economy
- The negative impact of the slave trade on the development of the Caribbean islands.

Glossary

Term	Meaning
Arable	Land that is suitable for growing crops.
Attorney	A person whose job it was to handle the legal and financial affairs of plantations on behalf of absentee plantation owners.
Bill of credit	A promissory note intended to circulate as money. Bills of credit were used to finance slave-trade voyages.
Bookkeeper	A person whose job it was to assist with the management of plantations. They would be responsible for recording the purchases of enslaved African people.

➔

Term	Meaning
British Empire	A term to describe the overseas territories that were historically controlled by the British crown.
Commonwealth	A political association of countries, many of which were formerly part of the British Empire.
Copper smelting	The process of applying heat to ore to extract copper.
Distillation	The process of heating a liquid until it becomes a gas, then making it liquid again by cooling.
Erosion	The gradual destruction and removal of rock or soil in a particular area by rivers, the sea or the weather.
Fermentation	The chemical process by which sugars in food or drink are turned into alcohol due to the action of yeast or bacteria.
Free people of colour or free coloureds	People of African or African–European descent who were not enslaved. They had either been born free or had purchased or been granted their freedom. Use of the term 'coloured' is outdated and inappropriate today.
Governor-General	The chief representative of the monarch in a Commonwealth country of which the British monarch is head of state.
Great House	The home of planters or attorneys who acted for absentee plantation owners. It was the location of those in authority on a plantation.
Indigenous	Originating or occurring naturally in a particular place.
Industrial Revolution	The period in the late eighteenth and early nineteenth century in which the introduction of power-driven machinery transformed the British economy. This led to a change in the way goods were produced, from human labour to machines.
Magistrate	A person who is appointed to act as a judge in law courts which deal with minor crimes or disputes.
Militia	A military force that is raised from the civilian population to provide support to a regular army in an emergency.
Molasses	A thick, dark brown juice obtained from raw sugar during the refining process.
Monoculture	The cultivation of a single crop in a given area.
Overseer	A person whose job it was to supervise the work of enslaved people on plantations.
Typhus	A disease caused by bacteria spread by lice, fleas or mites.

Chapter 3

The experience and resistance of enslaved people

The aim of this chapter is to explore what life was like for enslaved people in the Caribbean.

It will examine the horrific living and working conditions for enslaved people on the sugar plantations and the methods used by enslavers to maintain control over their enslaved workforce.

It will discuss other forms of slave labour on the Caribbean islands, such as the work that enslaved people were forced to do in the towns.

Finally, it will explore the ways in which enslaved people resisted on plantations, including everyday acts of resistance and attempts to overthrow the whole system of slavery itself. It will also highlight the ways in which enslavers responded to the fear of revolt by enslaved people.

Together, this will allow you to respond to questions from Key issue 3: The experience and resistance of enslaved people.

Link to the assessment

National 4 and 5

Key issue 3: The experience and resistance of enslaved people

- Living conditions on the plantations
- Working conditions on the plantations
- Terror on the plantations
- Other forms of slave labour on the Caribbean islands
- Resistance on the plantations
- Fear of revolt

! Note

Key issue 3 in the SQA course specification is called 'The captive's experience and slave resistance.' As highlighted in the Introduction, the term **'slave'** suggests that slavery was somehow a natural condition, whereas the word **'enslaved'** acknowledges that people were forcibly placed and held in the condition of slavery.

Similarly, the SQA course specification makes reference to **'discipline'** on the plantations. **'Terror'** is a more appropriate term to describe the brutal methods that enslavers used in their attempts to maintain control over enslaved people, and is used here.

Background

Upon arrival in the Caribbean, captives were sold and transported to plantations. These were large estates with fields for growing tropical crops such as sugar, cotton and coffee. As you learned in Chapter 2, the main crop grown on the Caribbean plantations was sugar. Enslaved people were forcibly put to work on the plantations to tend and harvest the crops. They were also forced to work as domestic servants.

Enslaved people on the plantations were listed alongside **livestock** in plantation accounts and inventories. They were treated as property and had no rights. The enslaved people would often be branded to show that they 'belonged' to their enslavers. Living and working conditions for enslaved people were horrific and they experienced cruelty on a daily basis.

Enslavers attempted to maintain control on the plantations by a combination of intimidation and incentives. White overseers were employed to supervise the forced work of enslaved people. They used the whip to ensure that enslaved people worked as hard as physically possible.

Enslaved people resisted their enslavement at every opportunity. They used covert forms of resistance such as working slowly, breaking tools or pretending to be ill. They also fought back against their enslavers through large-scale uprisings. The most famous of these is the Haitian Revolution, which you will learn about later in this chapter.

Tacky's Revolt

One significant example of resistance that falls outside our time period is Tacky's Revolt. Tacky's Revolt was a large-scale act of resistance by enslaved people that took place in Jamaica in 1760. It was led by a fugitive enslaved African called Tacky.

During the course of the revolt, hundreds of enslaved people attacked plantations. They killed around 60 white people and set fire to crops and sugar works. Eventually, Tacky was captured and beheaded. Over 500 other freedom fighters either died in battle, took their own lives or were executed as a warning to others. A further 500 were transported from the island as a punishment.

While Tacky's Revolt could not be used to gain credit in questions for this topic, it is of interest as background to this chapter because it undoubtedly influenced the resistance that took place between 1770 and 1807, and beyond.

Slave labour on the Caribbean islands was not confined to the plantations. Enslaved Africans were also forced to work in a variety of jobs such as dock workers and domestic servants in the towns.

As a result of the mass transportation of captive Africans to the Caribbean, black people outnumbered white people on the islands, sometimes by large numbers. This created a climate of fear among the white people, which resulted in harsh laws and measures designed to control the enslaved populations.

3.1 Living conditions on the plantations

In this section, you will examine the following:

o housing
o clothing
o diet
o health
o dangers faced by women.

3.1.1 Housing

Enslaved people lived in 'slave villages' on the plantations (Figure 3.1). These were collections of inadequate houses built at a distance from the Great House, close to the fields. It was common for enslaved people to have to build their own homes. These homes would usually be small cottages with thatched roofs and earthen floors. They contained a limited amount of furniture.

There are few traces of slave villages still visible today. Unlike the homes of the enslavers, which were made of stone, the wooden huts of enslaved people have long since disappeared.

Figure 3.1 A stone replica of an 1820s slave hut at Tyrol Cot Heritage Village, Barbados

The source below is a description of housing of enslaved people on a plantation, as observed by Olaudah Equiano.

Source 3.1

Their huts, which ought to be well covered, and the place dry where they take their short repose, are often open sheds, built in damp places; so that, when the poor creatures return tired from the toils of the field, they contract many disorders, from being exposed to the damp air in this uncomfortable state, while they are heated, and their pores are open.

Olaudah Equiano (1789) *The Interesting Narrative of the Life of Olaudah Equiano, or Gustavus Vassa, The African*

3.1.2 Clothing

Enslaved people would usually receive one or two sets of clothing per year. Those who worked in the Great House might be given more. Clothing for enslaved men generally consisted of shirts and trousers, while enslaved women wore shifts and petticoats. In some cases, enslaved people were simply given pieces of cloth to wrap around their body. You learned in the previous chapter that a coarse woollen fabric known as 'Welsh plains' or 'Welsh cotton' was sent to the Caribbean to be used as clothing for enslaved people. The historian Chris Evans has calculated that around 5 yards of this cloth was allocated to each adult. This is approximately 4.5 metres – not very much, considering how long it had to last. This fabric was popular because it was both durable and cheap.

3.1.3 Diet

Enslaved people ate a nutritionally deficient diet. In most places in the British Caribbean, small plots of land were given to enslaved people so that they could grow vegetables and fruit, for example, **yams**, **plantains** and bananas. It was common for enslaved people to be given a day in the week to work on their plots of land.

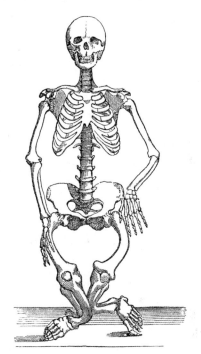

The crops grown by enslaved people were supplemented by imports from overseas such as pickled herring or salted cod from Britain. The over-reliance on imports could lead to shortages and hunger at certain times of the year. Droughts and hurricanes were also frequent and would result in the destruction of food crops. As a result, the diet of the enslaved people was of poor quality leading to conditions such as **rickets** and **scurvy**, which are caused by a lack of vitamins.

Figure 3.2 A human skeleton showing the telltale bow legs caused by rickets

3.1.4 Health

The poor diet, coupled with the exhausting nature of work on the plantations, severely weakened enslaved people. They were vulnerable to diseases such as **yaws**, smallpox and the '**bloody flux**' (dysentery). Other diseases included **dropsy** and '**dirt-eating**'. Dirt-eating was a craving to eat dirt, especially clay. It has been suggested that dirt-eating was connected to the nutritional deficiencies that enslaved people experienced as a result of their poor diet.

On the larger islands, plantations would usually employ doctors on a visiting or annual basis. However, on the smaller islands, doctors were not always available. Nor were these doctors always formally qualified. Many enslaved people who fell ill relied on the care of a fellow enslaved person who had some experience of health care. Larger plantations might have a 'hospital', sometimes known as a 'sick house' or 'hot house', where a white doctor would visit.

The poor diet and harsh working conditions resulted in a loss of **fertility** for women. In the mid-eighteenth century, about half of the enslaved women in the Caribbean never bore a child.

For children who were born into slavery, life expectancy was low. In early nineteenth-century Trinidad, the average life expectancy for an enslaved person born into a plantation was 17 years. Many enslavers were wealthy enough to be able to afford to work enslaved people to death and simply import new captives to replace those who died.

In the following source, the historian Randy Browne discusses the high mortality rates in the Caribbean.

Source 3.2

Historians have long known that Caribbean slave societies were death traps. African captives who did not die during the forced migration from the African interior to the coast, which consumed between 5 and 40 per cent of all captives, or during the notorious Atlantic crossing, which claimed at least 10 per cent more, usually succumbed within a few years of arrival in the West Indies, victims of a lethal combination of unrelenting work, a hostile disease environment, inadequate nutrition, and physical violence. Children born under slavery fared little better, with most infants dying well before their first birthdays.

R. M. Browne (2017) *Surviving Slavery in the British Caribbean*

3.1.5 Dangers faced by women

CAUTION: SENSITIVE CONTENT

Enslaved women faced specific dangers on the Caribbean islands. In a society dominated by white men, black women found themselves in a particularly vulnerable position. Sexual abuse of enslaved women by white men was common. Enslaved women could not refuse or consent to sex with white men. Enslaved women might be forced to have sex with their enslaver or with his visiting white neighbours and friends. If the women attempted to resist, they would face severe punishments.

Some enslavers viewed forced sex with enslaved women as a means of increasing the enslaved population of their plantations. It was not uncommon for enslavers to have children by enslaved women. These children would be born

Note

It was not until 1826 that rape of an enslaved woman became a crime in Jamaica. According to the journalist Alex Renton, no white man was ever punished for rape in Jamaica during the entire slavery period.

Consent could not be present in sexual interactions between enslaved women and their enslavers. Enslaved women did not have the freedom to make the choice to have sex.

with enslaved status, although they might receive certain privileges. Historians believe that many enslaved women tried to exercise some control over childbearing by obtaining substances that could be used to terminate a pregnancy, or by using other methods of contraception.

The precarious position of enslaved women is illustrated by the case of Thomas Thistlewood. Thistlewood was first an overseer then a plantation owner in Jamaica between 1750 and 1786. During this period he kept a diary in which he recorded the violence and rape that he inflicted on dozens of enslaved women. He was by no means an isolated example. Across the Caribbean, countless numbers of enslaved women suffered similarly.

Key fact summary

Living conditions on the plantations

Housing for enslaved people was basic and contained only a limited amount of furniture.

Enslaved people received one or two sets of clothing per year, made of coarse fabric.

→

Enslaved people ate a nutritionally deficient diet, supplemented by fruit and vegetables grown on small plots of land.
The poor diet and lack of nutrients made enslaved people more vulnerable to disease and conditions such as rickets and scurvy.
Life expectancy of enslaved people was low and mortality rates were high.
Enslaved women suffered sexual abuse at the hands of white men.

Activities

1 a) Read the information about living conditions for enslaved people on the plantations. Summarise the key points using the following headings:
  - Housing
  - Clothing
  - Diet
  - Health
  - Dangers faced by women.

You may wish to present your points in the form of a table, as shown below. You should aim to write several points under each heading.

Housing	Clothing	Diet	Health	Dangers faced by women

b) Use the information from your table to write a detailed paragraph about living conditions for enslaved people on the plantations.

2 a) Read Source 3.1. In this source, Olaudah Equiano gives a description of the housing of enslaved people on a plantation. What does he say about the houses?

b) Read Source 3.2. In this source, the historian R. M. Browne talks about mortality on the plantations. What reasons does he give to explain why mortality rates were so high for enslaved people?

3.2 Working conditions on the plantations

The majority of enslaved people on sugar plantations were forced to work in the fields. Others were made to work in the mill or boiling house. There were also artisans, tradesmen and blacksmiths. In the Great House, enslaved people were forced to work as domestic servants in roles such as cooks, maids or nannies.

In this section you will explore the working conditions of enslaved people on the plantations. This will include:

- field work
- the role of drivers
- work in the mill and boiling house
- the role of domestic servants
- other jobs on plantations.

3.2.1 Field work

On sugar plantations, labourers were required to sow, tend and harvest the sugar cane. This was back-breaking work that would be both physically and mentally exhausting.

The sugar crop was planted in the fields that were part of the plantation estates. When the cane was ripe, the enslaved labourers were forced to cut it by hand with **machetes**. The cut sugar cane would then be loaded onto carts and taken to the mill and boiling house to be processed.

Enslaved field labourers worked from dawn until dusk in the hot Caribbean sun. They were supervised by a white overseer, and they would be whipped or beaten to make them work harder.

The historian James Walvin describes the typical working day on a sugar plantation in Jamaica:

Source 3.3

The slave quarters were roused about 4.00 A.M. by a bell or conch shell (the conch shell was also the instrument used to rally rebellious slaves). Slaves were in the fields, depending on local custom, by 5.00 or 6.00 A.M. Jamaican slaves had breakfast in the field at nine, an hour and a half lunch break at midday, before labouring on to 6.00 P.M. All told, Jamaican field slaves worked twelve hours a day, those on the smaller islands ten hours, though the number of hours declined in the early nineteenth century.

J. Walvin (2001) *Black Ivory: Slavery in the British Empire*

Gangs

Enslaved people worked in gangs, with tasks allocated according to age and strength:

- The First Gang contained the strongest, healthiest people. They were forced to do the heaviest work, for example, digging, planting, cutting, carrying and loading.
- The Second Gang was composed of weaker people. They were forced to do jobs such as removing weeds or clearing the mill floor of its crushed cane.
- The Third Gang was made up of the very young or the very old. They were given the lightest work. Children were made to work in the fields from an early age. They did tasks such as carrying grass to the cattle and simple field jobs such as hoeing around the cane shoots.

Pregnant women

Pregnant women were made to work until the final month of their pregnancy and went back to work in the fields very soon after giving birth. The harsh working conditions presented risks to both the mother and her unborn child. Miscarriages were common and infant mortality rates were high. During the eighteenth century, over 80 per cent of the infants of enslaved mothers died within the first nine days of life. Death in childbirth was also a very real possibility. As you learned earlier in this chapter, doctors were not always available to treat enslaved people, especially on the smaller islands. Pregnant women often relied on the care of a fellow enslaved person who acted as midwife.

'Seasoning'

Captives who arrived from Africa were severely weakened by the journey. For this reason, enslaved people from Africa were often 'seasoned' for three years, receiving extra food and lighter work. 'Seasoning' was a psychologically traumatic time for captives, who found themselves in an unfamiliar and brutal environment, separated from family and friends and denied their freedom. Estimates suggest that at least a quarter of captives died within this period.

3.2.2 The role of drivers

Enslaved men could be appointed to the role of driver. Drivers had the job of keeping other enslaved people at work and carrying out punishments as directed by the overseer or enslaver. One visitor to St Kitts in the late eighteenth century noted that the driver carried two whips, one short and one long, as he supervised the work of enslaved people in the fields.

The specific role given to the drivers meant that they avoided the most physically demanding tasks, such as planting and cutting the sugar cane. They were also given better food and clothing and often better housing. As a result, most drivers lived longer than enslaved field labourers.

Mary Prince was an enslaved woman who was born into slavery in Bermuda. She was the first known black woman to share her experiences of slavery. In her book, *The History of Mary Prince, a West Indian Slave*, published in 1831, she describes a conversation with a driver, who she met at a prayer meeting:

Figure 3.3 An engraving of a slave driver forcing an enslaved woman with a young child back to work

Source 3.4

The husband of the woman I went with was a black driver. His name was Henry. He confessed that he had treated the slaves very cruelly; but said that he was compelled to obey the orders of his master. He prayed them all to forgive him, and he prayed that God would forgive him. He said it was a horrid thing for a ranger to have sometimes to beat his own wife or sister, but he must do so if ordered by his master.

Mary Prince (1831) *The History of Mary Prince, a West Indian Slave*

3.2.3 Work in the mill and boiling house

On sugar plantations, in addition to the field work, enslaved labourers were used to process the cut sugar cane. This was a highly skilled and dangerous job.

Once the sugar cane was cut, it needed to be processed quickly or the juice would ferment and spoil.

- The cut sugar cane was brought to the mill (Figure 3.4) by cart or donkey. Inside the mill, the enslaved workers fed the cane through wooden or metal rollers to crush it and extract the juice.
- The juice from the mill was then taken to the boiling house. Here it was boiled until it started to crystallise. The boiling had to be continuous, and the boiling sugar had to be carefully ladled from one boiling pan to another. The boiler would test the sugar with his elbow or by rubbing the hot syrup between his fingers.
- The boiling house would be unbearably hot, and the hours were long, especially at harvest time. During the harvest period, the enslaved people in the mill and boiling house typically worked for 24 hours per day to process the sugar crop.
- The work was exhausting, and accidents were common as conditions in the mills were so dangerous. An enslaved person with a machete would stand beside the enslaved labourer who fed cane into the mill, ready to cut off their arm if it became trapped.

Figure 3.4 The ruins of a sugar mill on St Kitts

3.2.4 The role of domestic servants

In the Great House, enslaved people would be forced to work as domestic servants, for example, as butlers, maids, cooks or nannies. In Barbados in 1788, estimates suggest that more than 25 per cent of the overall enslaved population was forced to work in these roles.

CAUTION: SENSITIVE CONTENT

Work in the Great House was less physically demanding than field work. However, enslaved domestic servants worked in closer proximity to the enslavers, which presented its own dangers. This was especially the case for women, who formed the majority of enslaved domestic servants. They were vulnerable to sexual abuse by white men. They could also be subjected to abuse by the white mistress in the home.

Mary Prince describes the treatment that she received at the hands of her female enslaver:

Source 3.5

The next morning my mistress set about instructing me in my tasks. She taught me to do all sorts of household work; to wash and bake, pick cotton and wool, and wash floors, and cook. And she taught me (how can I ever forget it!) more things than these; she caused me to know the exact difference between the smart of the rope, the cart-whip, and the cow-skin, when applied to my naked body by her own cruel hand. And there was scarcely any punishment more dreadful than the blows I received on my face and head from her hard heavy fist. She was a fearful woman and a savage mistress to her slaves.

Mary Prince (1831) *The History of Mary Prince, a West Indian Slave*

3.2.5 Other jobs on plantations

Other jobs on plantations included roles for craftsmen such as carpenters, masons and blacksmiths. There were also keepers of livestock and carters, whose job was to transport cargo around the island. Larger plantations might also have **distillers** and **coopers**.

Sexist attitudes towards women in this period meant that enslaved women were not able to become skilled or semi-skilled workers, and only enslaved men worked as coopers, carpenters, masons or blacksmiths.

Skilled workers such as carpenters and blacksmiths were valued for the additional economic benefits that their work brought to their enslavers. They were often better fed and given better clothing and housing. They were also not as closely supervised as the enslaved field labourers and tended to live longer, healthier lives compared to those of their non-skilled fellow enslaved workers.

Key fact summary

Working conditions on the plantations
Enslaved people in the sugar fields worked from dawn until dusk in the hot sun.
A gang system was used to allocate tasks according to age and strength.
Drivers had the jobs of keeping other enslaved people working and of carrying out punishments.
In the mill, the enslaved workers fed the cane through wooden or metal rollers to crush it and extract the juice.
Enslaved workers in the boiling house boiled the sugar until it started to crystallise.
Enslaved people were forced to work as domestic servants for their enslaver.
Skilled enslaved workers such as blacksmiths and carpenters were often treated better and lived longer than field workers.

Activities

3 a) Read the information about working conditions on the plantations. Choose one of the headings from this section to research:
   - Field work
   - The role of drivers
   - Work in the mill and boiling house
   - The role of domestic servants
   - Other jobs on plantations.

b) Write a one-minute talk explaining the main points. Your teacher may check to ensure there is a spread of headings across the whole class.

c) Your teacher will divide your class into two groups. Each group should form a circle, with one group making an inner circle and the other group making an outer circle. You should face each other, standing opposite a classmate.

Take it in turns to exchange your information with each other for approximately one minute. Give your classmates a red, amber or green rating and at least one suggestion for information they might have included.

➜

The inner circle then rotates clockwise, and the outer circle rotates anticlockwise. The new pair repeats the process.

The rotation continues until you have all had the opportunity to share information with at least four classmates.

4 Use the information in this section and the section about living conditions to make notes about the experience of enslaved women on the plantations. You might choose to present your findings as a report or digital presentation.

You might choose to do additional research for this task.

3.3 Terror on the plantations

CAUTION: SENSITIVE CONTENT in Section 3.3

Using this information in your assessment

You can use the information in this section to answer questions that ask about 'Discipline on the plantations.'

Enslavers recognised that there was a strong possibility that the enslaved people on the plantations would try to resist. Black people outnumbered white people overall on the Caribbean islands, especially on the plantations. Enslavers, therefore, devised harsh methods of maintaining control over their enslaved workforce.

3.3.1 Branding

One method of maintaining control was an attempt by enslavers to strip enslaved people of their identity. This included branding them and giving a new name to captive Africans as a way of showing that they were now 'owned'. Branding was a common practice in the Caribbean. It involved burning a mark into the skin of an enslaved person. Brand marks were often the initials of the enslaver (Figure 3.5). Enslaved people might be branded on the chest, shoulder or face.

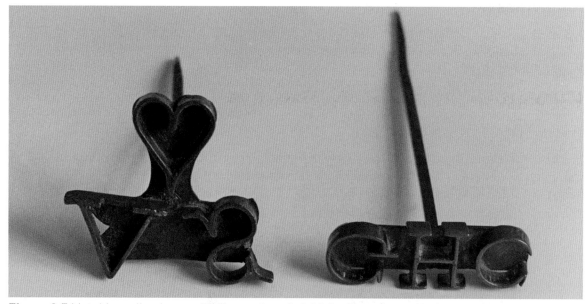

Figure 3.5 Metal branding irons with the enslaver's initials. Branding was also used as a punishment on the plantations.

3.3.2 Punishments

Violence was used on a regular basis on the plantations, both as a threat and as a punishment. Whipping was routinely used to make enslaved people work harder in the fields, but people would also be flogged as a form of punishment. There were other brutal punishments for even the smallest 'crime'. For example, the Reverend Henry Cooper, a visitor to Jamaica, recalled his white host nailing an enslaved female domestic servant to a tree by her ear for breaking a plate.

Formal executions and public punishments of enslaved people were specifically designed to act as a warning to others. If an enslaved person escaped and was recaptured, they could be hanged or have a limb cut off. For example, in Barbados, being absent for 30 days or more meant death. Enslavers also used attack dogs to pursue fugitives.

For other so-called 'crimes', enslaved people could be punished by being transported to another island, having their ears cut off, their nose slit or their face branded.

Figure 3.6 This plaque in Bridgetown, Barbados, marks the spot of 'The Cage', which was used as a temporary prison for captured fugitives until their enslavers could come and collect them

Olaudah Equiano describes witnessing multiple examples of the brutal treatment of enslaved people by their enslavers:

Source 3.6

One Mr. D___, told me he had sold 41,000 negroes, and he once cut off a negro-man's leg for running away … Another negro-man was half hanged, and then burnt, for attempting to poison a cruel overseer.

Olaudah Equiano (1789) *The Interesting Narrative of the Life of Olaudah Equiano, or Gustavus Vassa, The African*

3.3.3 The legal system

White society in the Caribbean was complicit in the violence that was inflicted on enslaved people on the plantations. White people controlled the legal machinery on the islands and white men acted as both jurors and judges in the local courts. It was rare for white people to be convicted of murdering enslaved people. If they *were* found guilty, they were more likely to simply be fined rather than jailed or executed. For example, in Barbados, an enslaver who killed an enslaved person would be fined £15. You will learn more about the legal system later in this chapter, in section 3.6.1 on slave codes.

3.3.4 Use of incentives

In addition to intimidation and the threat of physical abuse, enslavers also used incentives to maintain control. For example, skilled enslaved workers and drivers might be given additional free time or extra food and clothing. The importance of this is highlighted by the historian Christer Petley, who argues:

Source 3.7

… by creating divisive hierarchies and ruling over them as petty tyrants, granting and removing privileges as they saw fit, slaveholders were able to play on the hopes and doubts of the enslaved people they exploited, deterring all but the most determined of rebels, and ensuring that challenges to white authority in Jamaica failed to destroy the system.

C. Petley (2018) *White Fury: A Jamaican Slaveholder and the Age of Revolution*

It is also important to recognise that control was maintained through the fact that enslaved people were physically exhausted by the work that they were forced to do on the plantations. As a result, many were often too weak to attempt overt forms of resistance.

Key fact summary

Terror on the plantations
Whipping was used to make enslaved people work harder in the fields.
Enslaved people were branded to show that they 'belonged' to their enslaver.

→

Enslaved people were given a new name by the enslaver in an attempt to rob them of their identity.
Public punishments were used as a method of intimidation and deterring acts of resistance by enslaved people.
Punishments could include physical mutilation or even death.
Enslavers used a mixture of intimidation and incentives to maintain control.
The exhausting nature of the work on plantations helped enslavers maintain control as enslaved people were often too weak to attempt overt resistance.

Activities

5 Make a list of all of the ways in which enslavers attempted to maintain control over enslaved people on the plantations.

6 Answer the following questions:

a) Why did enslavers feel it was important to devise methods of maintaining control over the enslaved people on their plantations?

b) What was the purpose of public punishments and executions of enslaved people?

c) What was 'The Cage'?

d) Why do you think it was rare for white people to be convicted of killing enslaved people?

3.4 Other forms of slave labour on the Caribbean islands

While the majority of enslaved people in the Caribbean were forced to work on plantations, there were also enslaved people in the towns. By the end of slavery, almost 10 per cent of the population of the Caribbean islands lived in the towns. In 1788, for example, Jamaica had a total population of just over 250,000 people. Just over 26,000 people lived in Kingston, which was Jamaica's largest port town.

White settlers in the towns used enslaved people as domestic servants. They would often pay them to find accommodation nearby. In Bridgetown, Barbados, almost 70 per cent of all females in the town were domestic servants.

Other jobs that enslaved people were forced to do in the towns included:

- dock workers, including work repairing ships and making ships' equipment
- skilled jobs such as gunsmiths, watchmakers, goldsmiths, painters, tailors, carpenters
- washerwomen
- workers in taverns and inns
- seamstresses
- butchers
- bakers.

3.4.1 Hiring out of enslaved people

In Barbados, enslavers benefited financially from hiring out enslaved people to do public labour such as building and repairing roads and public buildings. They would be given £25 if the enslaved person they hired out died while involved in this work.

CAUTION: SENSITIVE CONTENT

Women were exploited by being hired out as forced sexual labour for passing sailors and soldiers. In Bridgetown, Barbados, the Royal Navy Hotel was a place where enslaved women were forced to provide sexual services to the sailors and military officers who were in port.

In her autobiography, Mary Prince describes being sold to an enslaver who lived in Grand Quay, a small town on Grand Turk Island. Grand Turk Island is part of the Turks and Caicos Islands. In 1799 this was **annexed** by Britain as part of the Bahamas. The salt industry developed on the islands. The labour for this industry was done by enslaved Africans who were trafficked directly from Africa or from other Caribbean islands. Mary Prince describes the work that she was forced to do in the salt ponds:

Source 3.8

I was given a half barrel and a shovel, and had to stand up to my knees in the water, from four o'clock in the morning till nine, when we were given some Indian corn boiled in water, which we were obliged to swallow as fast as we could for fear the rain should come on and melt the salt. We were then called again to our tasks, and worked through the heat of the day; the sun flaming upon our heads like fire, and raising salt blisters in those parts which were not completely covered. Our feet and legs, from standing in the salt water for so many hours, soon became full of dreadful boils, which eat down in some cases to the very bone, afflicting the sufferers with great torment. We came home at twelve; ate our corn soup, called *blawly*, as fast as we could, and went back to our employment till dark at night.

Mary Prince (1831) *The History of Mary Prince, a West Indian Slave*

The experience of enslaved people in urban areas differed from that of enslaved people on the plantations. In the towns, enslaved people were less easily supervised and controlled than those who lived on the plantations. They could experience a degree of independence. Fugitives from the plantations might try to reach the towns, in the hope of blending in with 'town slaves' or with the community of 'free coloureds'.

Key fact summary

Other forms of slave labour on the Caribbean islands
Enslaved people were forced to work in the towns as domestic servants.
Enslaved people were used in a variety of roles in the ports, including as dock workers.
Enslaved people were forced to work as skilled tradesmen, such as gunsmiths and tailors.
Enslaved people were forced to work in the taverns and inns.
Enslaved women were hired out as forced sexual labour for passing sailors and soldiers.
Enslaved people in the towns were often less closely supervised than those on the plantations.

Activity

7 Read the information about other forms of slave labour in the Caribbean islands. Summarise what you have learned using the following words and phrases in your answer:

towns	seamstresses
domestic servants	butchers
dock workers	bakers
skilled jobs	forced public labour
washerwomen	Royal Navy Hotel
taverns and inns	salt industry.

3.5 Resistance on the plantations

Resistance on the plantations could take the form of running away (fugitivity), acts of everyday resistance or attempts to overthrow slavery itself. This section will cover:

o covert forms of resistance
o fugitivity
o overt forms of resistance
o the Haitian Revolution
o difficulties of attempting overt resistance.

3.5.1 Covert forms of resistance

Enslaved people resisted in a number of ways on the plantations. Everyday resistance could include:

o doing a job slowly or poorly
o pretending to be ill
o stealing
o breaking tools
o setting fire to crops
o killing livestock
o poisoning the food and drink of their enslavers.

Enslaved people also resisted by attempting to maintain various African traditions and folk stories, or by attempting to maintain the languages of the regions of Africa from which they came. They found ways to communicate through song and music by using hidden codes in the words or meanings of their songs. This could include using music to mock and ridicule their enslavers.

Enslaved people maintained their own religious beliefs, for example Islam, or African spiritual beliefs such as **obeah**. Obeah was viewed with intense suspicion by enslavers, who feared that it might be used against them. Large numbers of practitioners of obeah were women. Some enslaved people also embraced Christian beliefs, for example Biblical references to enslaved people gaining their freedom.

3.5.2 Fugitivity

Enslaved people could resist by attempting to escape. At the Codrington plantation in Barbados, this was so common that one expense line on the plantation's annual budget included 'rewards for the return of runaway slaves'.

Those most likely to escape the plantations were skilled enslaved people and those who were referred to as 'coloured'. This is partly because they could go to the towns and blend in more easily with the community of 'free coloureds' and 'town slaves'. Many more men than women escaped.

Many left temporarily to visit loved ones or friends on neighbouring plantations. They could also attempt to join communities of former enslaved people such as the **Maroons**.

Newly arrived Africans were most likely to try to escape, but they were usually recaptured. By contrast, enslaved people who had survived for longer on the plantations, or who had been born on the islands, had more chance of success as fugitives. On larger islands such as Jamaica, they could hide in the inland forests. In some colonies, fugitives could attempt to reach other islands by sea.

3.5.3 Overt forms of resistance

The late eighteenth and early nineteenth centuries saw a surge in overt forms of resistance by enslaved people across the Caribbean and the wider Americas.

- During the eighteenth century there were more than a dozen major uprisings in Jamaica alone.
- There was a revolt on British-owned Tobago in 1774.
- There was a further revolt on the island of Grenada in 1795.
- There were also numerous plots that did not turn into full scale acts of resistance. In the 1790s, for example, the British feared unrest among the enslaved communities in Dominica, St Lucia, St Vincent and Grenada, in some cases involving indigenous peoples such as the Kalinago.

Leaders of resistance often came from among the elite, for example, drivers and skilled workers. Overt resistance was usually unsuccessful as the enslavers had access to military resources, including guns.

Maroons

The Maroons were primarily Africans who had escaped from plantations and lived in the mountains, free from British rule. The name 'Maroons' comes from the Spanish word *cimarron*, which means 'wild' or 'untamed'.

In 1739, the Maroons signed a treaty with the British. This gave the Maroons some land and in return they promised to return any fugitive enslaved Africans who tried to join them. However, the treaty did not put a stop to rebellions and in Jamaica in 1795, the British faced a rebellion from the Maroons. The Maroons used guerrilla tactics to raid plantations and attack the British forces.

The revolt was defeated but it took the British more than half a year of fighting and cost them £500,000. The British also suffered heavy casualties. Nanny was the leader of the Maroons in the early eighteenth century (Figure 3.7).

Figure 3.7 Nanny of the Maroons

3.5.4 The Haitian Revolution

The most significant and influential act of overt resistance by enslaved people in the Caribbean was the Haitian Revolution of 1791–1804.

In 1791, a large group of enslaved people from multiple plantations rose up on the French colony of Saint-Domingue, on the Caribbean island of Hispaniola. The freedom fighters attacked plantations and set fire to fields, mills and boiling houses. At various points they fought the British, the Spanish and the French, all of whom wanted control of the colony.

Many of the freedom fighters of the Haitian Revolution had been born in Africa. This meant that many of them had served in African armies prior to their enslavement and arrival in Saint-Domingue. They were able to use their experience of warfare to their advantage.

Figure 3.8 Toussaint L'Ouverture was a Haitian general and leader of the Haitian Revolution

The main leaders of the Haitian Revolution were Toussaint L'Ouverture (Figure 3.8) and, later, Jean-Jacques Dessalines (Figure 3.9).

L'Ouverture was captured by the French in 1802 and died in captivity on 7 April 1803.

Despite this setback, by the end of 1803, the French had been defeated, and on 1 January 1804, General Dessalines declared the Republic of Haiti.

Figure 3.9 Jean-Jacques Dessalines was a leader of the Haitian Revolution and the first ruler of an independent Haiti

Saint-Domingue

While the colony of Saint-Domingue was not part of the British Caribbean, the Haitian Revolution is important for a number of reasons:

- The British had attempted an invasion of Saint-Domingue in September 1793, expecting an easy victory. The small expeditionary force of 560 soldiers, which included a 'corps of black slaves' brought from Jamaica, managed to take control of some military posts, but by 1794 their advance had stalled. Thousands of British soldiers were sent to Saint-Domingue, but they were unable to defeat the freedom fighters. Large numbers of British soldiers died in battle and from disease. The British were forced to evacuate the island completely in 1798.
- The success of the Haitian Revolution caused some people in Britain to question whether it was worth trying to maintain slavery in the Caribbean if this could only be achieved with violence.
- As you will explore further in the next chapter, the Haitian Revolution is an important example of the role played by enslaved people themselves in bringing about the end of the trade in enslaved people and, ultimately, slavery itself.
- The Haitian Revolution was unique in that it was the only example of large-scale resistance by enslaved people that resulted in the defeat of a European power and the end of slavery on a Caribbean island. It remains the only successful revolt by enslaved people in recorded human history.
- The Haitian Revolution undoubtedly influenced further resistance by enslaved people in the Caribbean in the period that followed.

The importance of the Haitian Revolution is highlighted by the historian Adam Hochschild, who states:

Source 3.9

In the minds of both slaves and their owners, the Haitian Revolution altered the idea of what was possible, and it therefore raised the stakes in all the struggles that followed. For the first time, whites saw a slave revolt so massive they could not suppress it, and for the first time, blacks saw that it was possible to fight for their freedom and win.

A. Hochschild (2005) *Bury the Chains: The British Struggle to Abolish Slavery*

3.5.5 Difficulties of attempting overt resistance

You have seen that enslaved people resisted their enslavers at every opportunity. Success, however, was not guaranteed. Overt forms of resistance were difficult and dangerous. There are a number of reasons for this:

- The armed response to large-scale acts of overt resistance by enslaved people meant that they were usually unsuccessful.
- Enslaved people knew that if they used violence in resistance against slavery, they would be met with violence in return. Many did not feel able to take this risk.
- There were harsh punishments for any acts of resistance.
- Public executions of leaders of resistance were designed to act as a deterrent to others.
- The work on the plantations was physically exhausting, which left many enslaved people too weak to attempt overt forms of resistance. They struggled simply to survive each day.

- It was difficult for those who escaped the plantations to stay free for long, especially on the smaller islands, because there was nowhere for them to go.
- Rewards were offered for the capture and return of fugitives.
- Enslaved people might decide to stay on the plantations if they had family they did not want to leave behind.
- Enslaved people were closely watched by their enslavers, which made it difficult to plan and co-ordinate resistance.

Key fact summary

Resistance on the plantations
Enslaved people could resist by using such methods as doing a job slowly or poorly or by breaking tools.
Fugitivity was a common form of resistance, but it was difficult for enslaved people to remain free for long.
There were a number of significant uprisings of enslaved people in the British Caribbean in the final decades of the eighteenth century.
The Haitian Revolution of 1791–1804 resulted in the overthrow of slavery in the colony of Saint-Domingue.
The success of the Haitian Revolution inspired other acts of overt resistance in the period that followed.
The armed response to overt acts of resistance by enslaved people meant that they were usually unsuccessful.

Activities

8 Imagine you are a journalist and you have been asked to investigate and report on the ways in which enslaved people resisted on the plantations.

Think about what sort of questions you might like to ask. You can use the headings from this section as a starting point:
- Covert forms of resistance
- Fugitivity
- Overt forms of resistance
- The Haitian Revolution.

You might also choose to do additional research into other aspects of resistance to slavery.

a) Find and note down evidence for each of the headings you have identified.

b) Now you need to plan your article. Make notes of what you are going to write in your report.

c) Write a first draft of your article. Your article should be structured and well organised with a main heading and paragraphs.

d) Read through your work carefully and mark any mistakes you spot with a green pen, then correct your work before handing it to your teacher.

9 Make a list of reasons why it was difficult for enslaved people to attempt overt forms of resistance on the plantations.

3.6 Fear of revolt

The prospect of overt resistance caused white settlers on the Caribbean islands to live in a state of fear. There were constant rumours of plots by enslaved people, especially in the period following the Haitian Revolution.

Fear was increased by the fact that individual plantations could be distant from other properties. In the mountainous inland regions, the houses of the enslavers were often built high on the slopes, in view of each other. This was so they could communicate at a distance in case of any trouble. Many of these houses were fortified, especially in the remoter parts of the islands, as James Knight, an enslaver in Jamaica, describes:

Source 3.10

Houses are built with stone & made Defensible with Flankers, having loop holes for Fire Arms & Ports for small carriage Guns, the windows and Doors being made Musquet proof; so that they are capable of making a good defence.

J. Knight (1737–46) *Natural, Moral, and Political History of Jamaica, and the Territories thereon Depending: From the First Discovery of the Island by Christopher Columbus to the Year 1746*

Black people outnumbered white people across the Caribbean islands. On the plantations of Jamaica, enslaved people might outnumber white people by ten to one. This created unease among enslavers and their families. Enslaved people were closely watched by white people on the plantations. The houses of the white overseers were usually placed above or near the slave village so that they could keep an eye on the captives.

3.6.1 Slave codes

Following the revolts, there were periods of heightened tension. This often led to colonial governments passing laws aimed at restricting the activities of enslaved people. These were known as slave codes.

Some examples of slave codes are shown below:

- On Antigua, any enslaved person who was a fugitive for a period of three months or more would suffer death, loss of limb or whipping.
- On Montserrat, any fugitive who was absent for three months or more would be executed as a criminal.
- On St Kitts, if an enslaved person were to be found away from their enslaver's plantation without a pass, they could be whipped.

News of large-scale resistance spread across the islands and was talked about in the Great Houses and overheard by enslaved domestic servants. Enslavers feared that their enslaved workforce might be inspired by the news of rebellions and attempt their own uprising. This was particularly the case after the success of the Haitian Revolution. A letter from a concerned enslaver in the British colony of Tobago in 1794 noted that many enslaved people now believed themselves to be 'equal to their masters'. He feared that they would soon come together to 'exterminate the proprietors in the colonies'.

On the other hand, fear of revolt did motivate some enslavers to argue that improving conditions for enslaved people on plantations might help to prevent rebellions. They argued that it would be safer for enslaved people to be born on the Caribbean islands rather than imported from Africa. Those who were taken from Africa had experience of being free, whereas it was suggested that those born into slavery could be more easily controlled.

Key fact summary

Fear of revolt
Black people outnumbered white people on the islands, which made enslavers uneasy.
Rumours of plots by enslaved people were common.
Enslaved people were closely watched by white people on plantations.
There were periods of heightened tension following acts of resistance such as the Haitian Revolution.
Slave codes were passed to control the enslaved populations.
Fear of revolt led some enslavers to argue that it was necessary to improve conditions on the plantations in order to prevent further rebellions.

Activities

10 Make a list of reasons why enslavers on the Caribbean islands feared revolt.

11 Describe the ways in which enslavers on the islands responded to the fear of revolt.

Summary

Life on the plantations was horrific for enslaved people. They were treated as property and subjected to cruelty and violence on a daily basis. Enslaved women frequently suffered rape and sexual assault at the hands of white men.

Work in the sugar fields and sugar works was exhausting and dangerous. Mortality rates were high as a result of the gruelling nature of the work and the vulnerability of enslaved people to diseases. Many were literally worked to death.

Enslaved people were forced to work in the towns in a variety of roles, including as dock workers and skilled artisans such as tailors and carpenters. Enslaved women were forced into sexual service in the ports.

Attempts at resistance were usually unsuccessful, but this did not deter enslaved people from fighting back – sometimes with violence. The success of the Haitian Revolution inspired other acts of resistance across the Caribbean.

The fear of revolt led some enslavers to suggest that improvements might be made in the conditions of enslaved people. It also inspired the first attempts to restrict the trade in enslaved people. You will explore these arguments further in the next chapter.

Activity

12 Create a set of revision notes for this chapter. You should ensure that your notes cover the following headings:
- Living conditions on the plantations
- Working conditions on the plantations
- Terror on the plantations
- Other forms of slave labour on the Caribbean islands
- Resistance on the plantations
- Fear of revolt.

Glossary

Term	Meaning
Annexed	To take possession of an area of land or a country, usually by force or without permission.
'Bloody flux'	The historical name for dysentery.
Cooper	Someone who makes or repairs wooden casks or tubs.
'Dirt-eating'	A compulsive eating disorder in which people eat non-food items such as dirt and clay. It is believed that this was linked to the nutritionally deficient diet of enslaved people.
Distiller	A person who makes alcoholic drinks through the process of distillation.
Dropsy	A historical term used to describe swelling caused by fluid retention.
Fertility	The ability to produce children.
Flog(ged)	To beat someone with a whip or stick as a punishment.
Livestock	Animals such as cattle and sheep which are kept on a farm.
Machete	A broad, heavy knife.
Maroons	Communities of former enslaved people who lived in the mountains of Jamaica, free from British rule. There were also Maroon societies in other parts of the Americas.
Obeah	An African spiritual belief that includes healing practices.
Plantain	A tropical fruit similar to a banana that can be cooked and eaten as a vegetable.
Rickets	A condition that affects bone development in children.
Scurvy	A condition resulting from a lack of vitamin C in the diet.
Yam	A starchy vegetable that grows underground.
Yaws	A highly contagious tropical infection of the skin, bones and joints.

FIG. IV.

Store Room *Store Room*

Chapter 4

The abolitionist campaigns

The aim of this chapter is to examine the reasons why the trade in enslaved people ended in Britain in 1807.

It will discuss the origins of the abolitionist movement and its increased support, both outside and within Parliament. It will examine the role of the MP, William Wilberforce, who campaigned for abolition inside Parliament over many years.

It will explore the arguments and methods used by the abolitionists to promote their cause, and the arguments and methods used by those who wished to keep the slave trade.

It will highlight the key role played by resistance to the trade by enslaved people. It will also discuss the importance of the writings of black abolitionists such as Olaudah Equiano, Ignatius Sancho and Ottobah Cugoano.

Finally, it will explore the impact of the French Revolution before assessing the reasons why the slave trade was eventually abolished.

Together, this will allow you to respond to questions from Key issue 4: The abolitionist campaigns.

Link to the assessment

National 4 and 5

Key issue 4: The abolitionist campaigns

- Origins of the abolitionist movement
- Increased support for the abolitionist movement outside and within Parliament
- The role of William Wilberforce
- Arguments of the abolitionists: Christian, humanitarian, economic
- Methods used by the abolitionists
- Attitudes and evidence of enslaved people and former enslaved people
- Resistance to the trade by enslaved people
- Opposition to the abolition of the slave trade
- The effect of the French Revolution
- The debate over reasons for the eventual success of the abolitionist campaign

Note

The SQA course specification makes reference to 'attitudes and evidence of slaves and former slaves', and 'resistance to the trade by slaves'. As previously discussed, the term 'enslaved people' is used here.

Background

Africans were the first to protest against transatlantic slavery. As you learned in the previous chapter, they resisted their enslavement wherever possible.

Prior to the period you have been studying, few people in Britain questioned the morality of the trade in enslaved people. But in the last decades of the eighteenth century, a campaign emerged that aimed to put an end to it completely.

There are many reasons why the slave trade was ended. These include the campaigns of religious groups such as the Quakers and the role of white **abolitionists** such as William Wilberforce and Thomas Clarkson. Also important was the work of black abolitionists such as Olaudah Equiano, Ignatius Sancho and Ottobah Cugoano, whose accounts of their personal experiences helped to highlight the cruelties experienced by enslaved Africans. Of particular significance was the impact of resistance by enslaved people who fought for their freedom. Finally, the role of women was crucial to the success of campaigns such as the sugar boycott.

Despite growing support for the abolitionist movement, there was an active campaign to maintain the trade and slavery itself. This was led by wealthy enslavers and merchants who feared the loss of their income. The slave trade also had powerful supporters in Parliament.

The campaign to abolish the trade in enslaved people eventually achieved success on 25 March 1807, when the Act for the Abolition of the Slave Trade received **royal assent** and became law.

 Note

The law of 1807 only ended the trade in enslaved people. Slavery itself was not abolished in the British Empire until 1833 and the enslaved people of the British Empire did not gain their freedom until 1838.

4.1 Origins of the abolitionist movement

It is important to understand how the movement to end the trade in enslaved people began. In this section you will explore:

- early opposition to the slave trade by religious groups such as the Quakers
- legal challenges to slavery
- the role of Thomas Clarkson
- the establishment of the Society for Effecting the Abolition of the Slave Trade.

4.1.1 Early opposition to the slave trade by religious groups

Early opposition to the trade in enslaved people came from religious groups who argued that slavery was morally wrong and incompatible with Christianity.

Quakers

The first religious group to openly criticise slavery was the **Quakers**. In 1671 George Fox, the founder of the Quakers, called on enslavers not to use cruelty towards enslaved people. He also argued 'that after certain years of servitude they should set them free'. In 1783, British Quakers formed a committee to campaign against slavery and the trade in enslaved people. Their activities included publishing anti-slavery literature and petitioning Parliament against the slave trade. They also visited schools such as Eton and Harrow to spread the anti-slavery message. These schools were selected because some of their pupils were the sons of wealthy enslavers. It should be noted that many early Quakers were enslavers, while others spoke out against the slave trade.

Methodists

Other religious groups also expressed opposition to the trade. **Methodism** became popular in Britain in the 1740s and 1750s. The founder of the Methodists, John Wesley, criticised the trade in enslaved people in his pamphlet, *Thoughts Upon Slavery*, which was published in 1774. In 1788, Wesley delivered a famous sermon in Bristol in which he spoke about the immorality of slavery (Figure 4.1). As explained in Chapters 1 and 2, Bristol was a major slave-trading port and many businesses based in Bristol made money from the trade.

Figure 4.1 An early twentieth-century painting depicting John Wesley preaching his sermon against slavery in Bristol in 1788

Anglicans

Some **Anglicans** also criticised the slave trade. In 1784, the Reverend James Ramsay published two pamphlets about slavery. Ramsay had previously been a ship's surgeon and therefore had knowledge of conditions on board slave ships. In his pamphlets Ramsay called for an immediate end to the trade in enslaved people.

4.1.2 Legal challenges to slavery

Legal challenges to slavery allowed abolitionists to question whether slavery itself should be recognised in Britain. One important case was that of Joseph Knight in 1778. Knight was an enslaved African who had been brought to Scotland from the Caribbean by his enslaver. Knight sought his freedom via first the Justices of the Peace Court in Perth and eventually the Court of Session in Edinburgh. Knight argued that, as slavery was not recognised in Scotland, the act of landing in Scotland made him a free man. The Court of Session ruled that Knight's enslaver 'had no right to [his] service for any space of time, nor to send him out of the country against his consent.' Knight was allowed to go free.

Also in Scotland, in 1770, when a plantation owner in Fife attempted to return an enslaved man named David Spens to the Caribbean against his will, local coal miners and salt pit workers raised money for Spens' legal defence. In the end, Spens' enslaver died before the judges had an opportunity to make a decision and Spens gained his freedom by default.

Granville Sharp

The figure who is most associated with early legal challenges to slavery and the slave trade is Granville Sharp (Figure 4.2). Sharp was a civil servant who took on a series of legal battles to try to prevent enslaved people being taken out of England by force. One significant case was that of James Somerset in 1772. Somerset's enslaver brought him from North America to Britain. Somerset escaped in 1771 but was recaptured and his enslaver tried to take him to Jamaica to be sold. Sharp employed lawyers to bring the case to court. The case led to a ruling by Lord Mansfield, the Chief Justice, that, 'No master ever was allowed here to take a slave by force to be sold abroad because he deserted from his service, or for any other reason whatever – therefore the man must be discharged.' Somerset was freed. Sharp also tried, unsuccessfully, to have the crew of the *Zong* (see pages 22–3) prosecuted for murder. Sharp became a founding member of the Society for Effecting the Abolition of the Slave Trade.

Figure 4.2 Granville Sharp used his knowledge of the law to fight legal battles against slavery

The role of Thomas Clarkson

Another important figure in the early days of the abolitionist campaign was Thomas Clarkson. Clarkson was the son of a **clergyman**. He first became interested in the trade in enslaved people when he entered and won a Latin essay competition at Cambridge University. The essay was on the subject of whether it was lawful to enslave men against their will. Clarkson translated his essay from Latin into English, and it was published in 1786. The essay attracted a lot of attention and allowed him to meet other abolitionists, including Granville Sharp.

Thomas Clarkson became a prominent campaigner against the slave trade. As you will learn later in this chapter, Clarkson travelled thousands of miles around Britain, speaking against the trade in enslaved people and gathering evidence of its cruelties.

Figure 4.3 Thomas Clarkson, who was a prominent campaigner against the slave trade

4.1.3 The establishment of the Society for Effecting the Abolition of the Slave Trade

One of the most significant moments in the birth of the abolitionist movement in Britain came on 22 May 1787. A meeting was held in a London book store and printing shop 'for the purpose of taking the slave trade into consideration'. Twelve men were present – nine Quakers and three Anglicans, including Thomas Clarkson and Granville Sharp. The meeting led to the founding of the Society for Effecting the Abolition of the Slave Trade.

The group had a decision to make: whether to aim for the abolition of slavery itself or just the slave trade. Ultimately the members of the Society wanted to see an end to slavery, but they initially decided to target just the trade itself, as they felt that this would increase their chances of success. They believed that they could persuade the public that the greatest suffering took place on the slave ships of the Middle Passage. They also thought that if the trade was abolished and the supply of captives was cut off, either the enslaved population of the Caribbean would eventually die out, or enslavers would be forced to treat enslaved people better.

In May 1787 Thomas Clarkson met the MP William Wilberforce. Clarkson asked Wilberforce to take on the political leadership of the movement. This gave the abolitionists a representative in Parliament.

Key fact summary

Origins of the abolitionist movement
The Quakers were the first religious group to openly criticise slavery.
Other religious groups such as Methodists and Anglicans argued that slavery was morally wrong.
Legal challenges to slavery helped to establish the principle that enslaved people could not be taken out of Britain by force.
Granville Sharp used his knowledge of the law to fight a series of legal battles against slavery.
Thomas Clarkson became involved in the campaign after he won an essay competition at Cambridge University.
The Society for Effecting the Abolition of the Slave Trade was founded in 1787.

Activities

1 Use the information in this section to create a timeline of the key moments in the early years of the abolitionist movement.

2 Work in small groups. Use the information in this section to produce a mini lesson for the rest of your class, educating them about the origins of the abolitionist movement.

Your teacher will allocate to you one of the headings from this section:
- Early opposition to the slave trade by religious groups
- Legal challenges to slavery
- The role of Thomas Clarkson
- The establishment of the Society for Effecting the Abolition of the Slave Trade.

Work with your group to prepare and deliver your mini lesson.

4.2 Increased support for the abolitionist movement outside and within Parliament

In this section you will examine how support for the abolitionist movement began to grow, both outside and within Parliament.

4.2.1 Increased support for the abolitionist movement outside Parliament

The campaign to abolish the trade in enslaved people attracted support from a wide range of people and groups across Britain, including religious groups, women and working people. The popularity of coffee houses as a place to discuss current issues encouraged ordinary people to talk about the slave trade.

Newspapers and pamphlets

There was a growth in literacy in this period, which meant that people could read newspapers and pamphlets to find out more about the issues highlighted by the abolitionists.

The increased interest in the issue of abolition can be seen in the number of articles about the slave trade that appeared in newspapers in this period. In the 33 months prior to October 1787, 15 items about the slave trade appeared in *The Times* newspaper, and only 4 of these related to abolition. In the 15 months beginning with October 1787, 140 items on the slave trade appeared, of which 136 related to the arguments over abolition.

Anti-slavery petitions

In 1785 the first anti-slavery petition to the House of Commons was sent from the town of Bridgwater in Somerset. Further petitions followed, including from towns such as Manchester that were benefiting financially from involvement in the slave trade (see page 9).

In 1806 the slave trade became a major election issue for the first time in some constituencies. Several candidates switched to the abolitionist side, recognising the strength of public support for the cause.

 Note

In the period we are studying, very few people in Britain had the right to vote. A survey conducted in 1780 revealed that the electorate in England and Wales consisted of just 214,000 people. This was less than 3 per cent of the total population at the time.

No women had the right to vote. The political system was not representative, and power lay in the hands of a wealthy male elite. Pressure from outside Parliament could therefore have only a limited impact on its own.

4.2.2 Increased support for the abolitionist movement within Parliament

Support for abolition within Parliament was important because an act of Parliament would be required to formally end the slave trade. The Quakers were active in trying to persuade MPs to support their cause. They paid the doorkeepers of both Houses of Parliament to give out anti-slavery pamphlets.

It took a number of years before Parliament eventually passed the anti-slave-trade bill. The table below shows some of the major events.

 Note

In the period we are studying, Parliament was made up of the House of Commons and the House of Lords. In order to become law, **bills** needed to pass in **both** Houses. The King then needed to give his assent.

At this time MPs were not paid a salary and therefore needed to have enough money to support themselves. This meant that MPs were generally wealthy white men, a number of whom had a financial stake in the slave trade.

Table 4.1 Major events in the timeline for the bill to abolish the slave trade

Year	Event(s)
1788	• Over 100 petitions against the slave trade were presented to Parliament. • A committee of the **Privy Council** was set up to investigate the slave trade. • William Pitt, the Prime Minister, stated his intention to raise the issue of the slave trade in the next session of Parliament. • Dolben's Bill was passed in Parliament to regulate conditions on the slave ships. This bill aimed to restrict the number of captives carried by the tonnage of the carrier. It also required every ship to have a doctor and to keep a register of deaths of captives and crew. The bill was weakened by amendments but passed in both the House of Commons and the House of Lords.

Year	Event(s)
1789	● The Report of the Privy Council committee enquiry into the slave trade was presented to both Houses of Parliament. ● William Wilberforce made his first speech in the House of Commons against the slave trade.
1791	● James Towne, a carpenter on slave ships, gave evidence to a **House of Commons Select Committee** on the slave trade. ● Parliament voted 163 to 88 against abolishing the slave trade.
1792	● A bill for abolition of the slave trade was passed in the House of Commons but was rejected by the House of Lords.
1796	● The abolition bill nearly passed. The margin was very close (four votes) and the bill would have carried if a group of sympathetic MPs had not gone to see a new comic opera, with tickets paid for by opponents of the bill. In the period that followed, the British Government was itself actively involved in purchasing enslaved Africans to supply soldiers for the British West Indies regiments, to defend the Caribbean islands against the French.
1806	● The Foreign Slave Trade Abolition Bill banned British subjects, shipyards, outfitters and insurers from participating in the slave trade to the colonies of France and its allies. This was popular because at this time Britain was at war with France. The bill passed. ● More than 2000 people in Manchester signed a petition in favour of the Foreign Slave Trade Abolition Bill.
1807	● The bill was passed and An Act for the Abolition of the Slave Trade became law.

Key fact summary

Increased support for the abolitionist movement outside and within Parliament
The campaign to abolish the slave trade gained support from a wide range of people and groups.
The popularity of coffee shops as a place to discuss current issues encouraged people to talk about the slave trade.
Newspapers began to publish articles about the slave trade.
Dolben's Bill was passed in 1788. This aimed to regulate and improve conditions on slave ships.
In 1789, William Wilberforce made his first speech in the House of Commons against the slave trade.
In 1792, a bill for abolition of the slave trade passed in the House of Commons but was rejected by the House of Lords.
In 1806, a bill was passed banning British subjects, shipyards, outfitters and insurers from participating in the slave trade to the colonies of France and its allies.
In 1807 An Act for the Abolition of the Slave Trade became law.

Activities

3 Create a timeline to show the key events outside and within Parliament that eventually led to the abolition of the slave trade in 1807.

4 Below you will find a list of words, phrases or names. Read the information about increased support for the abolitionist movement outside and within Parliament. Create a set of questions that can only be answered by the words in the list.

working people	Bridgwater
coffee houses	1806
literacy	act of Parliament
fifteen	Dolben's Bill

4.3 The role of William Wilberforce

The campaign within Parliament is most closely associated with William Wilberforce (Figure 4.4). Wilberforce was the son of a wealthy merchant. In 1780 he became MP for Kingston upon Hull, and later represented the whole of Yorkshire.

Convincing Parliament

In 1780 there were 558 MPs in the House of Commons. By the time of the abolition of the slave trade in 1807, this figure had increased to 658, with the addition of MPs from Ireland following the Act of Union of 1800. Wilberforce needed to convince his fellow MPs to back his bills for the abolition of the slave trade.

By the time Wilberforce met Thomas Clarkson in 1787, he had already begun to educate himself about slavery. He opposed it for moral and religious reasons. Wilberforce became the leader of the abolitionist campaign inside Parliament. He was a close friend of Prime Minister William Pitt, which gave him additional influence.

Figure 4.4 William Wilberforce was an MP and prominent opponent of the slave trade

In 1788, Wilberforce was ready to raise the issue of the abolition of the slave trade in Parliament. However, he became ill and the slave trade debate was postponed. Dolben's Bill passed in the same year.

Impact of the French Revolution

In 1789, Wilberforce spoke for three and a half hours to set out the case against the trade in enslaved people. The House of Commons decided to hold its own hearings about the slave trade and abolitionists felt hopeful of gaining support for their cause. Unfortunately, at that moment the French Revolution began in Paris. The focus of the British government shifted to concern about the possible impact of the revolution on Britain and preoccupation with the subsequent war with France. As you will see later in this chapter, the French Revolution had a negative impact on the abolitionist campaign.

Wilberforce's determination

Wilberforce was important in the campaign to abolish the slave trade because of his role in attempting to persuade MPs to back his bills. He was a powerful speaker, and in his speeches he made use of evidence collected by Thomas Clarkson which highlighted the cruelties of the trade.

Wilberforce was hampered in his efforts by many factors, including personal illness, the revolutions in France and Haiti, the war with France and social problems at home. His opponents were also well organised and influential. Nevertheless, he displayed determination and he put forward a bill to end the slave trade each year for 18 years until the eventual success of the campaign in 1807.

Key fact summary

The role of William Wilberforce
William Wilberforce was the representative of the abolitionist campaign within Parliament.
Wilberforce made his first speech against the trade in enslaved people in the House of Commons in 1789.
Wilberforce put forward a bill to end the slave trade each year for 18 years.
Wilberforce used the evidence gathered by Thomas Clarkson to highlight the cruelties of the trade in enslaved people.
Wilberforce was a close friend of the Prime Minister, William Pitt, which gave him some influence.
Wilberforce experienced periods of illness, which hampered his efforts to persuade Parliament to end the slave trade.

Activity

5 Use the information in this section to create a profile of William Wilberforce. You should focus on his contribution to the campaign to abolish the slave trade. You might choose to do additional research for this task.

4.4 Arguments of the abolitionists: Christian, humanitarian, economic

Abolitionists put forward many arguments against the slave trade. You will examine each of these in turn:

- Christian arguments against the slave trade
- humanitarian arguments against the slave trade
- economic arguments against the slave trade.

4.4.1 Christian arguments against the slave trade

You have seen that Quakers were early opponents of the slave trade. Other religious groups were also active in the abolition campaign, including Methodists, Anglicans and the Church of Scotland. Both Granville Sharp and Thomas Clarkson were Anglicans, while Wilberforce was an **Evangelical**.

Religious groups argued that it was morally wrong to deprive God's subjects of the opportunity to live a free life. They believed that all men were equal in the eyes of God and that slavery was therefore incompatible with Christianity.

In 1774, John Wesley, the founder of Methodism, wrote:

> ### Source 4.1
>
> Liberty is the right of every human creature, as soon as he breathes the vital air. And no human law can deprive him of that right, which he derives from the law of nature.
>
> **J. Wesley (1774) *Thoughts Upon Slavery***

Christian groups believed that they had a responsibility to campaign against slavery. They were able to mobilise their members and congregations to help them spread the anti-slavery message.

4.4.2 Humanitarian arguments against the slave trade

During the eighteenth century, the **Enlightenment** movement promoted ideas of freedom, progress, tolerance and brotherhood. These ideas seemed incompatible with slavery. As the French philosopher, Rousseau, wrote in his publication *Du Contrat Social* (1762), 'The words *slave* and *right* contradict each other, and are mutually exclusive.'

In 1789, the *Declaration of the Rights of Man and of the Citizen* was published in France. Article 1 of the Declaration stated that all 'men are born and remain free and equal in rights'. While the Declaration did not explicitly mention slavery, this provided a further argument for abolitionists.

The Enlightenment influenced **humanitarian** arguments against the slave trade. Abolitionists argued that if the trade were ended, this would lead to better treatment of enslaved people who were already in the Caribbean.

A key argument that appealed to the British public was the belief that abolition of the trade in enslaved people might save the lives of British seamen. The brutal treatment of sailors was revealed in the evidence given to Parliament.

4.4.3 Economic arguments against the slave trade

The slave trade was hugely profitable and economic arguments were used by those who wished to keep slavery. Abolitionists also used economic arguments to campaign against the slave trade.

In 1787, Thomas Clarkson presented economic arguments to the founding members of the Society for Effecting the Abolition of the Slave Trade. Clarkson stated his belief that if the slave trade were ended, normal trade with Africa and the Caribbean could flourish, which would open up new opportunities overseas for British goods. Britain would also gain access to cheap markets for the raw materials that were needed by industry. Clarkson believed that the trade in people could be replaced with the trade in goods between Britain and Africa. On his travels around Britain, Clarkson used a collection of products from Africa, including African foodstuffs and textiles. He hoped to demonstrate that these products could be traded instead of people.

Thinkers of the time also questioned the economics of the slave trade. In his book *The Wealth of Nations*, which was published in 1776, the economist Adam Smith stated his belief that slavery was economically inefficient. He wrote:

Source 4.2

... it appears ... from the experience of all ages and nations ... that the work done by freemen comes cheaper in the end than that performed by slaves.

A. Smith (1776) *The Wealth of Nations*

Olaudah Equiano put forward the argument that if the trade in enslaved people were to be abolished, the population of Africa would increase, and this would encourage a growing demand for trade with Britain. He argued:

Source 4.3

If the blacks were permitted to remain in their own country, they would double themselves every fifteen years. In proportion to such increase will be the demand for manufactures. Cotton and indigo grow spontaneously in most parts of Africa; a consideration this of no small consequence to the manufacturing towns of Great Britain. It opens a most immense, glorious, and happy prospect; the clothing, &c. of a continent ten thousand miles in circumference, and immensely rich in productions of every denomination in return for manufactures.

Olaudah Equiano (1789) *The Interesting Narrative of the Life of Olaudah Equiano, or Gustavus Vassa, The African*

Key fact summary

Arguments of the abolitionists: Christian, humanitarian, economic
Christian groups argued that all men were created equal in the eyes of God and therefore slavery was wrong.
Christian groups believed they had a moral responsibility to campaign against the slave trade.

Humanitarian arguments against the slave trade included the belief that, if the trade were ended, planters would have to treat enslaved people better.

Enlightenment ideas about freedom and brotherhood seemed incompatible with slavery.

Economic arguments against the slave trade included the belief that the abolition of the slave trade would open up new opportunities for trade of British goods overseas.

Economists such as Adam Smith argued that slavery was economically inefficient.

Activities

6 Copy and complete the table below to show the main arguments used by the abolitionists. You should organise these under the headings 'Christian', 'Humanitarian' and 'Economic' arguments against the slave trade.

Christian arguments against the slave trade	Humanitarian arguments against the slave trade	Economic arguments against the slave trade

7 Use the information in this section to write a speech that presents the main arguments against the slave trade.

In addition to the Christian, humanitarian and economic arguments outlined above, you might also choose to include what you have learned already about the conditions experienced by enslaved people in slave factories, during the Middle Passage and on the plantations of the Caribbean.

4.5 Methods of the abolitionists

Abolitionists used a variety of methods to raise awareness of their campaign. These included:

- public meetings, lectures and debates
- evidence gathered by Thomas Clarkson
- first-hand accounts by enslavers
- production and distribution of pamphlets, leaflets, books and diagrams
- creation of merchandise to promote the anti-slavery message
- gathering signatures on petitions to send to Parliament
- the campaign to boycott sugar produced using slave labour.

4.5.1 Public meetings, lectures and debates

Abolitionists held lectures, public meetings and debates in towns across the country. Thomas Clarkson was a popular speaker at these. In February 1788, there were seven debates on the abolition of the slave trade in London alone. This was half of all public debates that were recorded in the city's daily newspapers that month. These public events were important in increasing awareness of the trade as ordinary people could attend and hear the first-hand experiences of those who had knowledge of slavery.

4.5.2 Evidence gathered by Thomas Clarkson

Between 1787 and 1794, Thomas Clarkson covered 35,000 miles on lecture tours around Britain. He carried with him diagrams, shackles and other instruments from slave ships to demonstrate the cruelties of the Middle Passage. He also took samples of African cloths to show that an alternative trade with Africa could be substituted for the slave trade.

In autumn 1787, Clarkson examined customs records of the main British slave-trading ports. He inspected a slave ship in Bristol and talked to people who had experience of life on board slave ships, including seamen and surgeons. He visited Liverpool and was threatened with assault on the quay. Clarkson received death threats and eventually took along Alexander Falconbridge as a bodyguard. Falconbridge was a former ship's surgeon who became an abolitionist. Falconbridge later revealed that he carried a gun for protection when he accompanied Clarkson.

William Wilberforce used Clarkson's evidence in his speeches against the slave trade in the House of Commons. Clarkson's evidence was important because it drew attention, not only to the suffering of African captives, but also to the brutal treatment of the crew on slave ships. This was an argument against the trade in enslaved people that appealed to the public.

The importance of Clarkson is highlighted by the historian James Walvin, who states:

Source 4.4

Clarkson was the man who helped to transform the public's vague and general sense that there was something wrong with the Atlantic slave trade into a powerful and focused national voice of widespread and strident opposition. Clarkson stirred up, and then channelled, this voice.

J. Walvin (2007) *A Short History of Slavery*

4.5.3 First-hand accounts by enslavers

Evidence from enslavers and former enslavers was used effectively by the abolitionists. The most famous of the former enslavers, who presented evidence of the cruelties of the trade, was John Newton. Newton had worked as a ship's mate and then as a captain of a number of slave ships. Later in life, he became an Anglican minister and began to campaign against the slave trade.

In 1788, Newton published a pamphlet, *Thoughts Upon the African Slave Trade*. The first edition sold out immediately. It was reprinted and sent to every Member of Parliament. Newton was also a powerful and popular speaker at public meetings about the trade in enslaved people.

4.5.4 Production and distribution of pamphlets, leaflets, books and diagrams

A key feature of the abolitionist campaign was its use of publicity to influence public opinion.

In the first year of the existence of the Society for Effecting the Abolition of the Slave Trade, the committee raised £2760.2s.7d. They spent over £1000 of this on the distribution of more than 80,000 pamphlets and books to spread the anti-slavery message. From 1788 onwards, the group arranged for some of the books and pamphlets to be translated into the languages of the other slave-trading countries – French, Portuguese, Dutch and Spanish. They also wrote letters to the King of Sweden and the King of Spain.

Diagram of the slave ship Brookes

The most famous diagram produced by the abolitionists was the drawing of the slave ship *Brookes* (Figure 4.5). This diagram showed how around 451 captives would be crammed into the ship's hold, although records show that on one voyage on the *Brookes*, 609 captives were in the hold. The diagram was printed by the Quaker printer, James Phillips. It appeared in books, magazines and newspapers, and thousands of copies were printed in poster form. Thomas Clarkson carried a copy with him on his tours around Britain.

Figure 4.5 Drawing of the slave ship *Brookes*. The *Brookes* diagram was used by abolitionists to illustrate the overcrowded conditions on board slave ships.

The diagram of the *Brookes* was important because it shocked the public. Clarkson said that the *Brookes* diagram 'seemed to make an instantaneous impression of horror upon all who saw it'. It was also visually striking, which was particularly effective in an age when many could not read. The historian Adam Hochschild discusses the importance of the diagram:

Source 4.5

Part of its brilliance was that it was unanswerable. What could the slave interests do, make a poster of happy slaves celebrating on shipboard? Precise, understated, and eloquent in its starkness, it remains one of the most widely reproduced political graphics of all time.

A. Hochschild (2005) *Bury the Chains: The British Struggle to Abolish Slavery*

4.5.5 Creation of merchandise to promote the anti-slavery message

In July 1787, the abolitionists commissioned pottery maker Josiah Wedgwood (himself an abolitionist) to produce medallions featuring the slogan 'Am I not a man and a brother' (Figure 4.6). These became popular among supporters of the cause. Thomas Clarkson described how, 'Some had them inlaid in gold on the lids of their **snuff boxes**. Of the ladies, several wore them as bracelets, and others had them fitted up in an ornamental manner as pins for their hair.'

Figure 4.6 A Wedgwood medallion. These could be worn as brooches and hair decorations. The image also appeared on sugar bowls and milk jugs and even as door handles.

Clarkson himself gave out 500 medallions to people he met on his travels. The Wedgwood medallions were important because they enabled ordinary people, in particular women, to publicly show their support for the campaign.

4.5.6 Gathering signatures on petitions to send to Parliament

Another method used by the abolitionists was the mass **petition**. In early 1788, between 60,000 and 100,000 signatures were gathered on petitions that were sent to Parliament calling for an end to the trade in enslaved people. In 1792 there were 561 such petitions. Parliament received more signatures on abolition petitions than it had ever received on any other subject.

Petitions were important because they demonstrated the strength of public opinion in favour of abolition. It was also significant that there were petitions even from areas that were benefiting economically from the slave trade, such as Sheffield and Manchester. Two-thirds of Manchester's male population signed a petition demanding an end to the trade in enslaved people.

Petitions were left for signature at town halls, printing shops, hotels, banks, coffee houses and pubs. Historians have calculated that between 1787 and 1792, 1.5 million people in Britain signed petitions against the slave trade (the national population in that period was around 12 million).

4.5.7 The campaign to boycott sugar produced using slave labour

As described in Chapter 2, sugar was Britain's largest import in the eighteenth century. In 1791 the abolitionists called for a **boycott** of slave-produced sugar. In doing this, they hoped to put economic pressure on the industries that depended on slave labour.

At the peak of the sugar boycott in 1792, more than 300,000 Britons refused to eat sugar that was grown by enslaved people. Many turned instead to sugar that was produced elsewhere, without the use of slave labour, for example India. In parts of the country, grocers reported sugar sales dropping by a third to a half in the space of a few months. Other workers refused to make products that would be used in the slave trade.

The sugar boycott was significant because it once again allowed ordinary people to demonstrate their support for the campaign and take practical action at a time when only a small proportion of the population could vote. The sugar boycott also allowed women across the country to participate in the campaign, as they were the main food purchasers for their households.

Figure 4.7 A sugar bowl with the words 'East India Sugar Not Made by Slaves' inscribed on the side

Key fact summary

Methods of the abolitionists
Public meetings, lectures and debates were held across the country.
Thomas Clarkson and John Newton were popular speakers at meetings.

| Thomas Clarkson travelled 35,000 miles around Britain, speaking against the trade in enslaved people and gathering evidence of its cruelties. |
| Former enslavers such as John Newton presented evidence of conditions on board slave ships. |
| The Society for Effecting the Abolition of the Slave Trade raised money to produce and distribute pamphlets, books and diagrams, including the diagram of the slave ship *Brookes*. |
| Josiah Wedgwood produced medallions featuring the slogan 'Am I not a man and a brother'. |
| Abolitionists gathered signatures on petitions that were sent to Parliament. |
| The sugar boycott was supported by thousands of Britons who refused to buy sugar that was grown by enslaved people. |

Activities

8 a) Use the information in this section to create a detailed mind map of all the different methods used by the abolitionists to campaign against the trade in enslaved people. You should ensure that you include information about the following:
- public meetings, lectures and debates
- evidence gathered by Thomas Clarkson
- first-hand accounts by enslavers
- publicity, including production and distribution of pamphlets, leaflets, books and diagrams
- creation of merchandise to promote the anti-slavery message
- gathering signatures on petitions to send to Parliament
- the campaign to boycott sugar produced using slave labour.

b) Which of these methods do you think was the most important? Give reasons for your answer.

9 Write the heading 'Methods of the abolitionists' on a very large sheet of paper.

Work in small groups. Each group will be allocated one of the methods used by the abolitionists to campaign against the slave trade. Each group should research their method and present the information in a creative way that can be added to the large sheet of paper. The aim is to create a wall display that gives information about the different methods used by the abolitionists.

4.6 Attitudes and evidence of enslaved people and former enslaved people

Personal accounts written by enslaved people and former enslaved people played an important role in informing the public about the experience of captive Africans.

Three men whose writings made a significant impact were Ignatius Sancho, Olaudah Equiano and Ottobah Cugoano.

Ignatius Sancho

Ignatius Sancho was born on board a slave ship and was brought to Britain as an infant (Figure 4.8). He became a writer, composer, shopkeeper and the first black person of African origin to be able to vote in British elections. His account of his experiences, *Letters of the Late Ignatius Sancho, an African*, was published in 1782. Sancho also wrote letters to the editors of newspapers calling for the abolition of the trade in enslaved people.

Figure 4.8 Ignatius Sancho

Olaudah Equiano

Olaudah Equiano was born in Essaka in what is now Nigeria (Figure 4.9). He was kidnapped by slave traders as a child and sent to Barbados. He was later brought to Virginia in the USA, where he was sold to a British naval officer. After more than a decade of enslavement, Equiano was able to buy his freedom. He settled in England and became involved in the campaign to abolish the trade in enslaved people. Equiano wrote a book about his personal experiences of slavery that became a bestseller and helped to educate people about the horrors of the trade.

Equiano's autobiography was published in 1789. The first edition of more than 700 copies sold out. It went through eight more editions in his lifetime and was translated into German, Dutch and Russian. Equiano also signed more than a dozen joint letters about slavery from groups of black men in London known as the 'Sons of Africa'. Equiano travelled around the British Isles, speaking against slavery and promoting his book.

Olaudah Equiano,
or
GUSTAVUS VASSA,
the African.

Figure 4.9 Olaudah Equiano

Ottobah Cugoano

Ottobah Cugoano was born around 1757 in what is now Ghana (Figure 4.10). In 1770 he was kidnapped and sold to European traders. Cugoano was transported to the Caribbean where he was forced to work in Grenada and other islands for nearly two years. Cugoano was brought to England by his enslaver in 1772 and subsequently gained his freedom. In 1787 he published a book called *Thoughts and Sentiments on the Evil and Wicked Traffic of the Slavery and Commerce of the Human Species*. This was the first English language abolitionist publication written by an African.

Cugoano argued that slavery was morally wrong. He demanded the complete abolition of slavery itself and the freeing of enslaved Africans. Cugoano's book went through at least three printings in 1787. It was translated into French and was revised for a new edition four years later.

Figure 4.10 Ottobah Cugoano

Who were the 'Sons of Africa'?

The 'Sons of Africa' was founded in 1786, one year before the Society for Effecting the Abolition of the Slave Trade. Members of this abolition society included Olaudah Equiano and Ottobah Cugoano. The Sons of Africa wrote or dictated letters calling for the abolition of slavery and the slave trade. In calling for the abolition of slavery itself rather than just the trade, the Sons of Africa went further than the Society for Effecting the Abolition of the Slave Trade.

The evidence of black abolitionists such as Equiano, Sancho and Cugoano was very important in bringing about the end of the trade in enslaved people. This is because their writings gave the British public a much deeper insight into the lived experience of captive people, both on the Middle Passage and on the plantations. They also helped to humanise African people in the minds of the British public.

Key fact summary

Attitudes and evidence of enslaved people and former enslaved people
Ignatius Sancho wrote letters to the editors of newspapers calling for the abolition of the slave trade.
Olaudah Equiano wrote a book about his personal experiences of slavery that became a bestseller.
Equiano travelled around the British Isles speaking about slavery and promoting his book.
Ottobah Cugoano published a book in which he argued that slavery was morally wrong. He demanded the abolition of slavery.
The 'Sons of Africa' was a group of black abolitionists in London who wrote letters about slavery.
The evidence presented by former enslaved people helped to educate the British public about the cruelties of the slave trade.

Activities

10 Read the information about Ignatius Sancho, Olaudah Equiano and Ottobah Cugoano. Use this information and additional research to create a fact file for each of these abolitionists.

   You should include information about their role in campaigning against slavery and the slave trade.

11 You may wish to do further reading of the thoughts and experiences of Ignatius Sancho, Olaudah Equiano and Ottobah Cugoano. For reference, the full titles of their books are:
   • Ignatius Sancho – *Letters of the Late Ignatius Sancho, an African*
   • Olaudah Equiano – *The Interesting Narrative of the life of Olaudah Equiano, or Gustavus Vassa, The African*
   • Ottobah Cugoano – *Thoughts and Sentiments on the Evil and Wicked Traffic of the Slavery and Commerce of the Human Species: Humbly Submitted to the Inhabitants of Great Britain.*

4.7 Resistance to the trade by enslaved people

One of the main reasons why the slave trade was ended in 1807 was the impact of resistance to the trade by enslaved people.

The table below shows some of the significant uprisings and planned rebellions during the period 1770–1807.

Table 4.2 Uprisings and planned rebellions during the period 1770–1807

Year	Event(s)
1769	● The First Carib War took place on St Vincent. This lasted until 1773.
1770	● A revolt of enslaved people took place at Courland Bay, Tobago.

Year	Event(s)
1771	● There was a revolt of enslaved people at Bloody Bay, Tobago.
1774	● There was an uprising of enslaved people at Queen's Bay, Tobago.
1776	● There was a plot in Jamaica.
1778	● There was a plot on St Kitts.
1785	● The First Maroon War took place on Dominica. This lasted until 1790.
1789	● Sporadic uprisings of enslaved people occurred in French-controlled islands in the Caribbean. These were inspired by the French Revolution.
1791	● In January an attempted uprising of enslaved people and 'free people of colour' was suppressed in British-controlled Dominica. ● In August the Haitian Revolution began in the colony of Saint-Domingue. ● Between 1791 and 1792 there was unrest of enslaved people in Jamaica as news spread of the Haitian Revolution.
1795	● The British feared revolts on St Lucia, Guadeloupe, Jamaica and Trinidad. ● There was an uprising in Dominica. ● The Second Maroon War began in Jamaica. This lasted into 1796. ● A major uprising took place on Grenada involving most of the enslaved people on the island. This lasted sixteen months. ● The Second Carib War took place on St Vincent. This lasted until 1796.
1796	● The Brigands' War took place on St Lucia, involving many enslaved people. This lasted until 1797.
1801	● A planned rebellion on Tobago was discovered.
1805	● Enslaved Africans in Trinidad planned a revolt against French-owned plantations.
1806	● There was a plot in St George's parish, Jamaica.

! Note

It should be recognised that resistance to slavery in the Caribbean continued after the abolition of the British slave trade in 1807. Large-scale acts of overt resistance by enslaved people in the period between 1807 and 1833 included:

● Bussa's rebellion in Barbados in 1816
● a rebellion of enslaved people in Demerara in 1823
● the 'Baptist War' in Jamaica in 1831–32.

These acts of resistance were important in bringing about the end of slavery itself in the British Caribbean.

Using this information in your assessment

Remember that the dates of this topic are 1770–1807. You should therefore ensure that any examples you give of resistance by enslaved people are taken from this period only. Although provided here for fuller context and understanding, do not include anything in your responses from after 1807.

4.7.1 Influence of the success of the Haitian Revolution on the abolitionist campaign

You learned in Chapter 3 about resistance in the colony of Saint-Domingue, which led to the establishment of the Republic of Haiti. The historian Claudius Fergus has argued that:

Source 4.6

... the Haitian Revolution, with its satellite revolts in the eastern Caribbean, was pivotal to the passage of abolition legislation from 1805 to 1807.

C. K. Fergus (2013) *Revolutionary Emancipation: Slavery and Abolitionism in the British West Indies*

The success of the Haitian Revolution was important to the abolitionist campaign for a number of reasons:

○ First, it gave encouragement to enslaved people across the Caribbean and the wider Americas and motivated them to continue their fight for freedom. For example, the historian Sudhir Hazareesingh has argued that the Haitian Revolution played a direct role in inspiring the nineteen conspiracies or revolts that took place on Cuba between 1795 and 1812.

○ Second, the Haitian Revolution led to a fear that if enslaved people were not freed, they might free themselves. When news of the revolt in Haiti reached London, stock prices fell and there was panic among enslavers everywhere. Successful acts of overt resistance such as the Haitian Revolution called into question whether it was worth trying to maintain slavery in the Caribbean if this could only be achieved with violence.

○ There was also an argument that it might be safer not to import new Africans to the Caribbean, especially if those Africans had experience of warfare, as was the case with the freedom fighters who fought in the Haitian Revolution. By 1804, a number of Jamaican plantation owners who held parliamentary seats began to offer qualified support for complete abolition. They argued that abolition of the slave trade could improve the safety of the British colonies and avoid the situation that had happened in Saint-Domingue.

On the other hand, acts of overt resistance by enslaved people alarmed both Caribbean plantation owners and politicians back in Britain, and made them fear what might happen if enslaved people were suddenly freed.

Key facts summary

Resistance to the trade by enslaved people
There were many plots and revolts by enslaved people in the period 1770–1807.
The success of the Haitian Revolution inspired other acts of overt resistance by enslaved people in the Caribbean and elsewhere.
News of the Haitian Revolution caused stock prices to fall in London.
Resistance to the trade by enslaved people caused enslavers to question the wisdom of importing new Africans to the Caribbean.
Enslavers began to wonder whether it was worth trying to maintain slavery in the Caribbean if this could only be done by using violence.
By 1804, some enslavers argued that abolition of the slave trade might improve the safety of the British colonies and prevent a similar revolution happening there.

Activity

12 Use the information in this section to create a timeline that shows the significant plots and uprisings of enslaved people in the Caribbean in the period 1770–1807.

   If space allows, you might choose to add the dates of the plots and uprisings to the timelines that you have already created for this chapter.

13 Based on what you have learned in this chapter, and in the topic as a whole, make a list of the reasons why resistance by enslaved people was so important in bringing about the end of the British slave trade in 1807.

4.8 Opposition to the abolition of the slave trade

Using this information in your assessment

You can use the information in this section to answer questions that refer to 'Arguments for the slave trade'.

Despite the growth in support for the abolitionist movement, it is important to remember that the trade in enslaved people had powerful supporters. These included merchants, admirals, landowners and members of the Royal family. In 1799, Prince William, the Duke of Clarence (and the future King William IV), made a speech in the House of Lords in support of slavery.

Those who opposed abolition put forward a number of arguments in favour of maintaining the slave system. These included:

o the racist belief that the trade of enslaved African people removed them from an 'uncivilised' continent and allowed them to live in the 'civilised' society of the Caribbean

o the argument that the slave trade was important in maintaining the naval supremacy of the United Kingdom. The Atlantic trade brought a huge expansion in the number of British ships and skilled crewmen, and acted as a training ground for the British Navy. It was also believed that sailors involved in the trade in enslaved people were able to develop immunities to tropical diseases

o the fear that Britain would lose out if the trade in enslaved people were to be abolished. Supporters of the slave trade argued that other countries would simply take over Britain's role and benefit financially from it

o the argument that thousands of British people would lose jobs which depended on the slave trade

o the argument that the availability of the products of slavery – tea, coffee, sugar, tobacco and cotton – would be put in jeopardy without the continued supply of slave labour to the Caribbean plantations.

The West India Committee

The West India Committee was founded in the eighteenth century to represent the interests of enslavers and merchants. During the period we are studying, the West India Committee was active in attempting to defend slavery and the trade in enslaved people.

The committee paid newspapers directly to print pro-slavery articles. They also printed 8000 copies of a propaganda pamphlet which falsely claimed that each enslaved family had 'a snug little house and garden, and plenty of pigs and poultry.'

Those who campaigned to keep the slave trade attempted to counter the sugar boycott by publishing a pamphlet claiming on medical authority that 'sugar is not a luxury, but ... a necessary of life; and great injury have many persons done to their constitutions by totally abstaining from it.'

Another example of pro-slavery propaganda was the play, *The Benevolent Planters*, which was published by Thomas Bellamy in 1789. The play attempted to portray a false, positive image of life for enslaved people on plantations.

Specific groups put forward their own arguments for retaining the slave trade.

This section will explore:

- the arguments of enslavers
- the arguments of Members of Parliament
- the arguments of cities
- the effect of the French Revolution.

4.8.1 Enslavers

Enslavers argued that plantations would be impossible to operate without a steady supply of new captives to replace those who died as a result of the harsh conditions in the Caribbean. They warned of mass rebellions in the Caribbean if the slave trade were to be ended. They also argued that enslaved people were property and that the rights of enslavers to their 'property' should be respected.

They claimed that conditions on the plantations were not as bad as abolitionists made out and even conducted tours of plantations in an attempt to show the 'best' quarters.

4.8.2 Members of Parliament

Supporters of the slave trade spent large amounts of money to make sure they were elected to Parliament where they could defend their interests. Several Members of Parliament (MPs) were absentee plantation owners and enslavers. It has been suggested that by the beginning of the 1780s, there were as many as 74 men in the House of Commons who had connections to the Caribbean. Many supporters of the trade in enslaved people were powerful and wealthy enough to be able to bribe other MPs to support them.

MPs for cities such as London, Bristol and Liverpool made speeches in Parliament opposing abolition. They argued that millions of pounds worth of property would be threatened by the abolition of the slave trade. They also claimed that the slave trade was necessary to provide labour on the plantations and that abolition would ruin the colonies.

There were also attempts to drag out inquiries before the House of Commons and House of Lords.

One MP who has been accused of deliberately trying to delay the abolition of the trade in enslaved people was Henry Dundas. In 1792, Dundas was Home Secretary. In that year, he introduced the word 'gradually' to the motion of Wilberforce in the House of Commons that called for immediate abolition of the slave trade. Historians have argued that this delayed abolition for fifteen years. As a result of the delay, from 1793, over 2000 further slave-trade voyages departed from British ports, carrying more than 583,000 African people into a life of slavery. Dundas was also involved in the government's purchase of enslaved Africans to supply the British West Indies regiments in the years after 1795.

4.8.3 Cities

There were petitions against abolition from cities with an obvious vested interest, such as Bristol, Liverpool and Birmingham. For example, in 1789, the traders of Bristol signed a petition against abolition. The petition was based on the claim that trade with the Caribbean and Africa constituted at least three-fifths of the commerce of the port of Bristol. Many other cities similarly feared a loss of income if the slave trade were abolished.

Employment was another factor used in their arguments. A good proportion of these cities' populations were employed by industries directly involved in the trade in enslaved people such as shipbuilding, or in industries that used the products of enslaved labour like sugar and cocoa.

4.8.4 Effect of the French Revolution

The French Revolution began in 1789, just at the time when the abolitionist campaign was gathering momentum.

> **What was the French Revolution?**
>
> The French Revolution was a period of radical political and social change in France that began in 1789 and lasted until the rise of Napoleon in the late 1790s. The monarchy was overthrown, and France became a Republic. Britain was at war with France for much of this period and also during the period of Napoleon's rule after 1799.

Historians argue that the French Revolution got in the way of abolition. There are a number of reasons for this:

- The British government became concerned about the possibility of revolution at home and in the colonies. This led to a fear of instability and a reluctance to make any major changes such as the abolition of the trade in enslaved people.
- Because of the fear of revolution spreading to Britain, public meetings of any kind worried the government. In 1795 the government passed the Seditious Meetings Act. This said that any public meeting of more than 50 people had to be authorised in advance by a magistrate. This made it harder for abolitionists to gather in large groups.
- Thomas Clarkson was open about his support for the French Revolution. Many people in Britain associated abolitionism with revolutionary ideas, which they viewed as dangerous.
- Abolitionists were fearful of being labelled **seditious**. Wilberforce was forced to publicly deny connections with the Jacobin Club of Paris, which was the most famous political group of the French Revolution.
- In 1793 the French king was executed, and Britain declared war on France. The British government became preoccupied with the war with France and had less inclination or time to consider the abolition of the slave trade.
- While Britain was at war, it needed ships and sailors to protect itself and its colonies. As we have seen, the slave trade was viewed as a valuable training ground for the Royal Navy.
- Britain also needed money to pay for the war with France. Supporters of the trade in enslaved people argued that abolition of the trade would result in a catastrophic loss of income.

In fact, the rise of Napoleon may have aided the abolitionists. Slavery was abolished in France in 1794 but Napoleon reinstated it in 1802. While Britain was involved in the Revolutionary Wars, opposition to the slave trade was viewed by some as unpatriotic. But now, to be anti-slavery could be seen as being anti-French and therefore more acceptable.

Key fact summary

Opposition to the abolition of the slave trade
The slave trade had powerful supporters in Parliament.
Enslavers argued that a steady supply of captives was needed to maintain the plantation system.
MPs argued that Britain would lose out financially if the slave trade was abolished.
Cities argued that jobs would be lost and industries would collapse if the slave trade was abolished.
The West India Committee spent vast amounts of money on pro-slavery propaganda.
The French Revolution hampered the efforts of the abolitionists to persuade Parliament to back Wilberforce's bills.

Activities

14 Copy and complete the table below to show the main arguments used by those who wanted to keep the slave trade.

General arguments against abolition	Arguments used by enslavers	Arguments used by MPs	Arguments used by cities	Effect of the French Revolution

15 Based on what you have learned from this section, make a list of reasons why it took so long to abolish the slave trade.

Which reason do you think was the most important? Explain your choice.

4.9 The debate over reasons for the eventual success of the abolition campaign

After many years of campaigning, the abolition movement achieved success when the bill for the abolition of the slave trade finally became law on 25 March 1807. There are a number of reasons for this, which we have explored in this chapter. This section will summarise the key reasons why the British trade in enslaved people was eventually ended in 1807. These include:

- public opinion
- parliamentary debate
- economic circumstances
- other reasons.

4.9.1 Public opinion

One key reason why the abolition campaign was successful was due to the effective campaign methods used by the abolitionists to capture the imagination of the public. This can be seen in the large numbers who supported the sugar boycott and in the popularity of anti-slavery merchandise, such as the Wedgwood medallions.

4.9.2 Parliamentary debate

Parliamentary debate was very important because an act of Parliament was required for the slave trade to be abolished. The MP William Wilberforce displayed determination in presenting his bills for abolition over a period of eighteen years, each failing until the passing of the Act for the Abolition of the Slave Trade in 1807.

4.9.3 Economic circumstances

It has been suggested that the trade in enslaved people was ended because it was no longer profitable. There are arguments both for and against this view:

On the one hand, it is true that by 1806, the price of sugar had fallen to a low point, and as a result, enslavers had less money to buy new captives from Africa.

On the other hand, it is also possible to argue that by the time of abolition, the slave trade, and plantation slavery itself, were still profitable:

- The sugar trade was very prosperous between the years 1790–99.
- In 1798, almost 150 ships (the highest number ever) left Liverpool for Africa.
- There were more sugar estates in Jamaica by the beginning of the nineteenth century than there had been in the 1770s.
- The duties on sugar and other imports from the Caribbean alone provided an eighth of the exchequer's income in 1807.
- The average profit per slave voyage was around 13 per cent in this period.
- At the beginning of the nineteenth century, over 30 per cent of British imports came from the Caribbean colonies.

Historians put forward the following views about the role of economic circumstances in the abolition of the slave trade:

Source 4.7

It is not easy to explain so profound a change in the ethics of a people. It used to be argued that slavery was abolished simply because it had ceased to be profitable, but all the evidence points the other way: in fact it was abolished despite the fact that it was still profitable.

N. Ferguson (2003) *Empire: How Britain Made the Modern World*

Source 4.8

The British economy appeared even more to depend either on slavery, or on slave-produced goods, in the first years of the nineteenth century than when the movement for abolition had been launched.

H. Thomas (1997) *The Slave Trade: The History of the Atlantic Slave Trade, 1440–1870*

Source 4.9

The current evidence simply does not sustain an argument that the British ended the slave trade for economic reasons.

J. Walvin (2007) *The Trader, The Owner, The Slave: Parallel Lives in the Age of Slavery*

4.9.4 Other reasons

There are many reasons why the British trade in enslaved people ended in 1807. These include:

- the role of religious groups such as the Quakers
- the role of white abolitionists such as Granville Sharp, William Wilberforce and Thomas Clarkson
- the role of former enslavers such as John Newton
- the successful campaign methods used by the abolitionists
- the role of black abolitionists such as Olaudah Equiano, Ignatius Sancho and Ottobah Cugoano
- the impact of resistance to the trade by enslaved people.

It is also important to recognise the role of women in bringing about the end of the slave trade. Women had few rights in eighteenth-century Britain, and they could not become MPs. Women were excluded from leadership of the abolition movement, but their support was crucial to the success of the campaigns. In particular, women played an important role in the sugar boycott because they were the main food purchasers for their households. Women also spoke in debates.

One notable female British abolitionist was Hannah More (Figure 4.11). She was a successful poet, playwright and campaigner. More was close friends with William Wilberforce and her poem, 'Slavery', published in January 1788, helped raise awareness of the cruelties of the trade.

Engraved by E. Scriven.

Hannah More

Figure 4.11 Hannah More was a notable female abolitionist. Women were important supporters of the movement. After the slave trade was abolished in 1807, women continued to campaign for the abolition of slavery itself.

As you learned in the previous chapters, enslaved women were also active in fighting against slavery, both during the Middle Passage and on the Caribbean plantations.

The importance of the role of women is highlighted by the historian David Olusoga, who argues:

Source 4.10

At certain times and in certain places they were the engine room of the movement. Traditionally confined to the domestic sphere, women brought anti-slavery politics into the home via the sugar boycott. It was women who did the most to promote and propagate that campaign which drew the mocking scorn of journalists and the engravers of satirical cartoons. The abolitionist movement, especially in its campaigns of the 1820s and 1830s, could not possibly have achieved what it did without their involvement.

D. Olusoga (2016) *Black and British: A Forgotten History*

Key fact summary

The debate over reasons for the eventual success of the abolition campaign
By 1807, public opinion shifted in favour of the abolitionist cause.
Campaign methods such as publicity, lectures and petitions helped to increase support for the movement.
Wilberforce's determination in presenting bills over eighteen years helped to sway Parliament.
Parliamentary debate was important because it was an act of Parliament that eventually ended the British trade in enslaved people in 1807.
Many historians do not believe that economic circumstances led to the abolition of the slave trade.
Religious groups played a role in the abolition of the trade in enslaved people.
White abolitionists such as Clarkson and Sharp contributed to the success of the abolition campaign.
The role of black abolitionists such as Sancho, Equiano and Cugoano was crucial in highlighting the cruelty experienced by enslaved people.
Resistance to the slave trade by enslaved people was one of the most important reasons why the slave trade was ended in 1807.
Women were important supporters of the movement.

Activities

16 a) Copy and complete the table on the following page. Use all the information from this chapter to complete the table to show the reasons why the slave trade was ended in 1807. You should include relevant facts for each factor.

b) Decide which factor you think is the most important. Be prepared to give reasons for your choice.

Factor	Key points to explain why this led to the abolition of the slave trade in 1807
The role of religious groups such as the Quakers	
The role of white abolitionists such as Granville Sharp, William Wilberforce and Thomas Clarkson	
The role of former enslavers such as John Newton	
The successful campaign methods used by the abolitionists	
The role of black abolitionists such as Olaudah Equiano, Ignatius Sancho and Ottobah Cugoano	
The impact of resistance to the trade by enslaved people	
The role of women	
Public opinion	
Parliamentary debate	
Economic circumstances	
Any other factors	

17 Use what you have learned in this chapter to plan an essay that answers the question:

'How important was the impact of resistance to the trade by enslaved people in bringing about the end of the slave trade in 1807?'

You should write this answer as a short essay, with an introduction, main paragraphs and a conclusion.

- Your introduction should state the factors that you will include in your essay (this will include the impact of resistance to the trade by enslaved people and other factors from the table above).
- The main part of your essay should include evidence that the impact of resistance to the trade by enslaved people was important in bringing about the end of the slave trade. It should also include evidence that other factors were important.
- Your conclusion should answer the question and give at least one reason to back up your judgement.

Summary

The issue of why the slave trade was eventually ended is debated by historians. It was certainly due to a combination of factors.

One of these was the role of Thomas Clarkson in gathering evidence of the horrors of the trade in enslaved people. Other significant factors included the work of Wilberforce in Parliament, the campaigns of religious groups such as the Quakers and the support of women. The evidence of former enslavers such as John Newton also shocked the public.

The contribution of black abolitionists was important in presenting to the public first-hand experiences of slavery. Enslaved people also played an important role in fighting for their own freedom through acts of overt resistance such as the Haitian Revolution.

The abolitionists used a variety of methods to raise awareness of their campaign. These included posters, books, diagrams and the creation of anti-slavery merchandise. The *Brookes* diagram helped to illustrate the cramped conditions for captives on the Middle Passage, while the sugar boycott demonstrated the strength of public opinion in favour of abolition.

It took a number of years to abolish the trade in enslaved people. Several factors got in the way, including the French Revolution, and the fact that the trade made so much money for Britain. The slave trade also had powerful supporters. Opponents of abolition spent vast amounts of money on pro-slavery propaganda in an attempt to convince the public that conditions on slave ships and plantations were not as bad as the abolitionists claimed.

When the bill for the abolition of the slave trade became law on 25 March 1807, abolitionists celebrated. However, this was not the end of the story. It is important to emphasise that the Act for the Abolition of the Slave Trade only ended the *trade* in enslaved people. As you have learned, slavery itself was not abolished in the British Empire until 1833 and the enslaved people of the British Empire did not gain their freedom until 1838. In addition, as was highlighted in Chapter 2, former enslavers received £20 million in compensation (in the currency value at that time) when slavery ended. This was equivalent to 40 per cent of the Treasury's annual income for that period. The bill was so enormous, it took until 2015 before it was paid off. The enslaved people themselves received nothing.

Activity

18 Create a set of revision notes for this chapter. You should ensure that your notes cover the following headings:
   - Origins of the abolitionist movement and its increased support outside and within Parliament
   - Role of William Wilberforce
   - Arguments used by the abolitionists
   - Attitudes and evidence of enslaved people and former enslaved people
   - Resistance to the trade by enslaved people
   - Opposition to the abolition of the slave trade
   - Effect of the French Revolution
   - Debate over reasons for the eventual success of the abolitionist campaign.

Glossary

Term	Meaning
Abolitionist	Someone who wanted to end the slave trade.
Anglicanism	A branch of the Church of England and other churches that share its doctrines, such as the Episcopal Church of Scotland.
Bills	A bill is a proposal for a new law.
Boycott	To refuse to buy a product (or service) as a means of expressing strong disapproval.
Clergyman	A minister or religious leader.
Enlightenment	The period in the eighteenth century in Europe when many people began to emphasise the importance of science and reason, rather than religion and tradition.
Evangelicalism	A Christian movement that arose in the eighteenth century.
House of Commons Select Committee	A committee within the House of Commons that is appointed to consider an issue. In this case, the issue of the slave trade.
Humanitarianism	A belief in improving people's lives and reducing suffering.
Methodism	An eighteenth-century Christian movement founded by John Wesley.
Petition	A formal written request, typically one signed by many people, appealing to authority in respect of a particular cause.
Privy Council	A body of advisers appointed by the monarch.
Quaker	A member of the Religious Society of Friends, a Christian movement founded by George Fox c.1650 and devoted to peaceful principles.
Royal assent	The final step required for a parliamentary bill to become law.
Seditious	Inciting or causing people to rebel against the authority of a state or monarch.
Snuff box	A small box for holding snuff (a scented, powdered tobacco).

Index